QUICK AND EASY
LOW-CARB RECIPES

Joanna White

Bristol Publishing Enterprises
Hayward, California

A **nitty gritty**® Cookbook

Printed in the United States of America.
ISBN: 1-55867-293-1

Cover design: Frank J. Paredes
Cover photography: John A. Benson
Food stylist: Susan Devaty
Illustrator: Grant Corley

CONTENTS

A SENSIBLE APPROACH TO LOW-CARB EATING

This book contains recipes suitable for those seeking a lower-carbohydrate approach to weight loss. Lower carbohydrate diets have resulted in reduced risk of heart disease, diabetes and cancer. The added advantage is weight loss, higher energy levels and feeling good about oneself. The idea of low-carbohydrate eating is to minimize refined-grain foods and sweets and replace them with protein-rich, high-fiber meals. This tends to normalize blood sugar levels and helps curb the impulse to binge. This book is divided into multiple categories—appetizers, salads, soups, eggs, entrees, vegetables, sauces and desserts. The recipes are generally high in protein and low in carbohydrates. Many dessert recipes are based on eggs because they are high in protein and do not require a large quantity of sugar. I am not a fan of allowing high fat in the diet—moderation is the key word. Some fat is necessary, but excess does not lend itself to a healthy lifestyle. Concentrate on learning how to cook healthy, tasty foods that are high in fiber and protein and you will live a longer, healthier and happier life.

REFINED AND UNREFINED CARBOHYDRATES

There are two general classes of carbohydrates: refined and unrefined. Refined carbohydrates are essentially refined sugars and refined flours, including: sugar, soft drinks, maple syrup, sweetened yogurt and any ingredient that ends with "ol" like sorbitol or "ose" like maltose or dextrose.

Unrefined carbohydrates are found in fruit, beans, potatoes, most vegetables, and in whole grains. These would include buckwheat, quinoa, whole grains including whole-grain bread, cereals and pastas.

Unrefined carbohydrates are healthier because they include soluble and insoluble fiber. Fiber is important for weight loss because it makes you feel full, so you have a tendency to eat less. Fiber also helps maintain good bowel function.

All carbohydrates are eventually converted by your body into glucose (blood sugar), which is our primary source of energy. It takes your body longer to convert protein into glucose and still longer to convert fat into glucose.

UNDERSTANDING THE GLYCEMIC INDEX

Not all carbohydrates are converted at the same rate. Researchers developed the glycemic index (GI), which ranks foods containing carbohydrates according to how quickly they raise your blood sugar within a 2- to 3-hour period after eating. The ranking index goes from 1 to 100 (100 being pure glucose).

Foods ranked 56 or above are considered high-GI because they spike your blood sugar. Foods ranked 55 or below are considered low-GI because the food is absorbed more slowly, thus causing a gradual raise of the blood sugar level.

Note: if you choose to eat a high GI food, try combining it with foods that are higher in protein and fat. This will slow down the rate at which the food raises the blood sugar.

Listed below are the more common foods and their Glycemic Index numbers.

BAKED GOODS

Angel food cake	67
Bagel	72
Bran muffin	60
Corn tortilla	70
Croissant	67
French bread	95
Graham cracker	74
Pumpernickel bread	41
Waffle	76
White bread	70
Whole wheat bread	69

CEREALS

All-bran	42
Cornflakes	84
Oat bran	55
Old-fashioned oats	59
Puffed rice	88
Shredded wheat	70

GRAINS

Barley	26
Brown rice	55
Bulgur	48
Cornmeal	68
Instant rice	91
White rice	68

PASTAS

Bean threads	26
Brown rice pasta	92
Gnocchi	68
Linguine	46
Macaroni & cheese	64
Spaghetti	41

LEGUMES

Baked beans (canned)	48
Green lentils	30
Kidney beans (canned)	52
Kidney beans (dried)	27
Pinto beans	45
Soybeans	18

DAIRY

Ice cream	61
Skim milk	32
Tofu frozen dessert	115
Whole milk	27

FRUITS

Apple	36
Banana	53
Cantaloupe	65
Cherries	22
Grapefruit	25
Grapefruit juice	48
Grapes	43
Mango	55
Orange	45
Orange juice	57
Pear	36
Pineapple	66
Pineapple juice	46
Plum	24
Raisins	64
Watermelon	72

VEGETABLES

Baked potato	85
Beet	64
Boiled new potato	62
Carrot	71
French fried potatoes	75
Fresh corn	59
Green peas	48
Instant mashed potatoes	83
Parsnip	97
Pumpkin	75
Sweet potato	54
Tomato	38

SNACKS

Chocolate	49	Soy milk	31
Corn chips	72	Sugar	65
Peanuts	14	Tortilla chips	74
Pretzel	83	Vanilla wafer	77
Rice cake	82		

GENERAL RULES FOR A LOW-CARBOHYDRATE DIET

1. *Eat More Whole-Grain Foods*

   a. Whole grains boost your fiber intake, which makes you feel full so you will have a tendency to eat less.

   b. Fiber-rich foods are generally loaded with nutrients that strengthen your immune system.

   c. Read labels, looking for the first ingredient to be a whole grain food. These would include: whole wheat, oats, whole-wheat pastas, brown rice, unpearled barley, etc.

   d. Buy low-glycemic index grains, such as pumpernickel bread. If you have a tendency to like breads too much, at least eat protein with your bread to slow down to fast absorption of the higher GI grains.

e. Try to limit your starches to no more than four servings per day (a serving is about ½ cup). Keep in mind that vegetables such as potatoes, corn, sweet potatoes, lima beans, lentils and beans are also starches.

2. *Eat More Vegetables and Fruits*

a. Choose fresh or frozen whenever possible. Canned foods have a tendency to have additives such as sodium and sugar.

b. Avoid breaded vegetables. These are generally high in carbohydrate, fat and sodium.

c. Try to eat mostly fresh, low-carbohydrate vegetables—these include most vegetables that are not on the hi-GI index list.

d. Strive to increase your servings of vegetables and fruits every day. Add more vegetables to your casserole. Try eating a little more salad with your meals. Keep cut raw vegetables in your refrigerator to snack on easily.

3. *Eat Lean Proteins and Healthy Fats*

a. Try to choose lean proteins like poultry, eggs, seafood, lean cuts of red meat, nuts, reduced-fat cheeses, etc.

b. Avoid fatty meats and cheeses. Choose the less fatty tenderloins and loins or roasts, game meats, lean hams, and extra-lean ground beef. Try using low-fat ground turkey and chicken in place of ground beef.

c. If you want to eat cold cuts, try to avoid the high-sodium variety and avoid fillers in the ingredients list.

d. Eat more fish. Fish is a good source of healthy fats like omega-3 and omega-6 fatty acids, which protect your heart. Eat more salmon, tuna, sardines, trout, halibut, cod and mackerel.

e. Eat more nuts and seeds, which contain the healthy fats. These include walnuts, flaxseeds, nut butters, nut oils and most types of nuts and seeds.

f. Use unsaturated fats as much as possible. Use mostly liquid oil such as olive and canola oil. Choose high-oleic oils whenever possible.

g. Avoid hydrogenated fats, like margarine and shortening. These are extremely high in trans fatty acids. They act like saturated fat in the body, which increases your cholesterol and increase your risk of heart disease.

4. *Try to Reduce Your Sugar Intake*

a. Eat less refined sugar whenever possible. Avoid soft drinks that are loaded with sugar. Get into the habit of drinking lots of water. Slowly decrease your intake of sugar products and replace them with healthier alternatives.

b. Avoid "low-fat" labels—these usually contain higher levels of sugar to compensate for the fat removed.

c. A quick calculation to determine the amount of sugar per serving is to divide the grams of sugar by 4 to determine how many teaspoons of sugar are in that serving size. If the label reads 16 grams, dividing by 4 means that there are 4 teaspoons of sugar per serving.

d. Avoid prepared foods that have any of the first few ingredients listed as corn syrup, invert sugar, high-fructose corn syrup, sucrose, dextrose, fructose, maltose, lactose, brown sugar or honey.

e. Limit your intake of milk because it is high in lactose (a simple sugar very similar to table sugar). If you are worried about calcium, increase your intake of calcium-rich foods like figs, collard greens and soy milk.

f. Eat low-GI fruit. As a general rule, eat the fiber-filled fruit instead of drinking the juice. Concentrate on fresh, unsweetened fruit as opposed to canned fruit.

g. There are only two types of artificial sweeteners that I like to use. Stevia is a natural herb that is up to 300 times sweeter than sugar. It has been extensively tested and has no negative side effects on the body. Splenda is a sugar that has been altered so it has no carbohydrates. Use the same quantity of Splenda as you would sugar.

5. *Watch Portion Control*

a. In the beginning, measure your foods to determine what is a true serving size.

   You can give yourself visual cues to help understand portions, such as ½ cup is about the size of a tennis ball, or 3 ounces of meat approximates the size of a deck of cards.

6. *Note Which Foods Start Your Cravings*

a. Foods like white bread, white rice and white pasta, or high-sugar drinks and desserts, can trigger your cravings.

b. These foods have a tendency to sabotage your efforts to change. You need to become aware of them so you can start making changes in your eating habits.

c. Avoid keeping these trigger foods in your house. Slowly start weaning these foods away from your life. When you do eat them, eat slowly and start reducing the quantity.

d. Keep healthy snacks prepared and available, so when you want something fast, the healthy alternative is easy to reach.

e. Plan ahead when socializing. Eat some high-protein foods before going to a party, or even bring some healthy munchies with you.

7. *Exercise Is Not a Dirty Word!*

a. Slowly start increasing your activity by taking walks. Start setting up meetings with friends that involve some form of exercise. You can walk around the lake and talk at the same time.

b. Look at fun ways to exercise—like joining a dance class or swim class. Or possibly take up bike riding or skating.

c. Get at least 30 minutes of some kind of exercise per day to begin a healthier lifestyle and start feeling good about yourself.

APPETIZERS

SUN-DRIED TOMATO AND GOAT CHEESE SPREAD   Makes 2 cups

Generally, this spread is served on crostini, or toasted bread slices, but you can serve this spread on whole-wheat bread or crackers. To really cut the carbohydrates, use slices of jicama or any firm vegetable instead.

1 cup chopped sun-dried tomatoes (not packed in oil)
3 tbs. olive oil
2 tbs. balsamic vinegar
$1/2$ cup pitted chopped kalamata olives
1 large jicama, or toasted bread rounds
8 oz. goat cheese
finely chopped fresh basil, optional

Place sun-dried tomatoes in a small bowl, cover with hot water and set aside to soak for 10 minutes. Drain, discarding liquid, and place tomatoes in a bowl along with oil, vinegar, and olives. Peel jicama and cut into $1/8$-inch-thick slices. Spread jicama slices with goat cheese, then with tomato mixture. If desired, sprinkle with basil.

SESAME AND ONION SPREAD

This simple recipe can be whipped together in minutes to serve when unexpected guests arrive. Serve with whole wheat crackers or toasted whole-grain bread. This spread can also serve as a topping for steamed vegetables or baked potatoes.

$\frac{1}{2}$ cup (1 stick) butter, softened
4 green onions, finely chopped
$\frac{1}{2}$ cup sesame seeds

In a small bowl, using a mixer, beat butter and green onions together. In a dry skillet, sauté sesame seeds over medium-high heat, stirring constantly, until seeds are well browned. Cool toasted seeds to room temperature, then combine them with butter mixture.

SPICY ROASTED MUSHROOMS

Hot chile oil, the secret ingredient in this dish, can now be found in most supermarkets. Add more chile oil if you really like it hot. Serve these mushrooms spread on whole-grain crackers or large thin slices of vegetables such as jicama or kohlrabi.

4 cups mixed sliced mushrooms (such as portobello, shiitake, oyster, button)
3 tbs. chopped shallots or onions
2–3 cloves garlic, mashed
salt and pepper to taste
1½ tbs. olive oil
6 oz. goat cheese
1 tsp. chile oil
pepper to taste
fresh or dried thyme leaves, for garnish

Heat oven to 400°. Combine mushrooms, shallots, garlic, salt, pepper and olive oil together and place in a shallow baking dish. Bake for 15 minutes until mushrooms are tender. Crumble goat cheese over mushrooms, sprinkle with chile oil, pepper and thyme and serve immediately.

CRISPY LEEKS

Servings: 4

This unique appetizer will offer something different to your guests. Consider sprinkling the leeks with shredded Parmesan cheese and some Italian herbs, or go spicy with a little chipotle spice or cayenne. There are endless variations to this simple appetizer.

2 medium leeks
2–3 tbs. olive oil
salt and/or herbs to taste

Heat oven to 400°. Remove the tough green tops of the leeks and discard. Split the leeks lengthwise and rinse well under running water to remove all sand. Cut the leeks lengthwise into long strips. Heat oil in a skillet over medium-high heat and sauté leeks for about 5 minutes, stirring frequently. Spread the leeks on a cookie sheet and bake for 15 minutes, stirring frequently, until leeks are very crispy. Sprinkle with salt and/or herbs of choice and serve immediately.

BAKED GOAT CHEESE AND GARLIC

I like to use elephant garlic in this recipe, but if it is not available, use 12 large garlic cloves instead. Serve on baguette slices, crackers or slices of crisp vegetables like jicama.

6 elephant garlic cloves
1 tbs. olive oil
2 tbs. butter
1 medium red onion
1½ tbs. brown sugar

12 oz. soft goat cheese
1 tbs. balsamic vinegar
salt and pepper to taste
¼ cup minced fresh basil

Heat oven to 350°. Peel garlic, place in foil or a small covered baking dish and drizzle with oil. Bake for 40 minutes (30 minutes if using regular garlic). Set aside to cool. Keep oven at 350°.

Melt butter in a large skillet over medium heat. Thinly slice onion and sauté for about 15 minutes until onion begins to brown. Stir in brown sugar and remove from heat. Place onion mixture in an 8-inch glass baking dish. Crumble goat cheese over onions. Sprinkle roasted garlic on top. Bake for about 20 to 25 minutes. Remove from oven, stir in balsamic vinegar and season with salt and pepper. Garnish with minced basil. Serve warm.

SUN-DRIED TOMATO DEVILED EGGS

Sun-dried tomatoes have become very popular these last few years. They give a whole new dimension to deviled eggs.

6 hard-cooked eggs, peeled
4 oz. sun-dried tomatoes packed in oil, drained
1/4 cup mayonnaise
1/4 cup sour cream, or cream cheese, softened
3/4 tsp. white wine vinegar
salt and pepper to taste
1 tbs. minced fresh parsley
slivered sun-dried tomatoes or fresh tomatoes, for garnish

Halve the eggs, reserve whites, and place yolks in a food processor workbowl. Add sun-dried tomatoes and process until chopped. Add mayonnaise, sour cream, vinegar, salt and pepper and pulse just to combine. Taste and adjust seasonings. Mound filling in egg white halves and sprinkle with parsley. Garnish each egg half with a sliver of sun-dried or fresh tomato.

CILANTRO AND ROASTED RED PEPPER DIP

Makes 2¼ cups

Sun-dried tomatoes come packaged dry "as is" or packed in oil. Do not use the oil version in this recipe or the mixture will result in a gooey mess! If you love spicy heat, add more jalapeños.

3 oz. sun-dried tomatoes (not packed in oil)
1 can (14 oz.) roasted red peppers, drained
3 cloves garlic, minced
1½ tsp. ground cumin
1 pickled jalapeño pepper, finely minced

1½ tsp. fresh lemon juice
¼ cup chopped fresh cilantro
¼ cup chopped green onions
4 oz. cream cheese, softened
salt to taste

Cover sun-dried tomatoes with hot water and soak for 30 minutes. Drain tomatoes, reserving 3 to 4 tbs. of the soaking liquid. In a food processor workbowl or blender container, puree sun-dried tomatoes, red peppers, garlic, cumin, jalapeño, lemon juice, cilantro and green onions. Add cream cheese and process until smooth. Taste and add salt if desired. Add enough of the reserved tomato soaking liquid to thin the mixture to desired consistency. Serve immediately or refrigerate until ready to use.

SUN-DRIED TOMATO STUFFED MUSHROOMS

Adding lemon juice to mushrooms keeps them from turning black. Instead of using the standard button mushrooms, try stuffing portobello mushrooms and cutting them into small wedges.

12 oz. sun-dried tomatoes (packed in oil)
2½ lbs. button mushrooms (about 24)
1 tsp. fresh lemon juice
⅓ cup chopped shallots or onions
1½ tsp. minced garlic

⅛ tsp. dried thyme
¼ cup heavy cream
salt and pepper to taste
⅓ cup shredded Parmesan cheese

Heat broiler. Drain sun-dried tomatoes, reserving ¼ cup of the oil. Chop tomatoes and set aside. Cut stems off mushrooms at the edge of the cap. Finely mince stems and set aside. In a small bowl, mix 2 tbs. of the reserved tomato oil with lemon juice. Brush the mushroom caps with oil mixture and place gill sides down on a broiler rack. Broil for about 2 minutes or until mushrooms are soft. Remove mushrooms from broiler and arrange them on a cookie sheet gill sides up. Heat oven to 350°. In a skillet, heat the remaining 2 tbs. tomato oil over medium heat and sauté shallots and garlic until soft. Stir in sun-dried tomatoes, mushroom stems, thyme, cream, salt and pepper. Cook, stirring occasionally, for 10 minutes, until mixture is thickened. Mound each mushroom cap with mixture and sprinkle with Parmesan cheese. Bake for 12 for 15 minutes until hot.

CHEESY RED ONIONS

You will need to make this recipe two days in advance to allow the flavors to develop. Serve on rye or pumpernickel bread or whole-grain crackers.

½ cup olive oil
2 tbs. fresh lemon juice
1 tsp. salt
½ tsp. sugar
1 pinch pepper
1 pinch paprika
2 cups sliced red onions
⅓ cup crumbled blue cheese

In a bowl, combine olive oil, lemon juice, salt, sugar, pepper and paprika. Add onions and cheese, cover and refrigerate for 2 days before serving.

PORK AND VEAL PÂTÉ

Servings: 6–8

The trick to making a good pâté is to weight it down with something heavy so the resulting loaf is condensed and easy to cut. If you choose not to use veal, substitute a good low-fat beef.

2 tbs. butter
1/2 cup finely minced onions
1/2 cup port wine or cognac
1 lb. pork, finely ground
1 lb. veal, finely ground

1/2 tsp. thyme
1 1/2 tsp. salt
1/8 tsp. pepper
1/4 tsp. ground allspice
2 garlic cloves, mashed

Heat oven to 350°. In a skillet over medium heat melt butter and sauté onions until soft but not brown. Remove onions from skillet and set aside. Add wine to skillet, increase heat to high and reduce by half. Place reserved onions, wine, pork, veal, thyme, salt, pepper, allspice and garlic in a bowl and stir until well combined. Place mixture in a 9 x 5-inch loaf pan and pack down to avoid air bubbles. Cover with foil. Set in a large pan. Pour boiling water in large pan to halfway up the sides of loaf pan. Add more boiling water while cooking to keep water at same level. Bake in lower third of the oven for 1 1/2 hours, until pâté has shrunk from the sides and juices are clear. Remove from oven and remove the foil. Place a heavy weight, such as a brick covered in foil, on the pâté and refrigerate for several hours. Cut into thin slices and serve.

SAUSAGE TERRINE (PÂTÉ)

This high-protein appetizer is delicious and versatile. Serve in slices with fresh whole-grain bread or even as a main dish (similar to meat loaf). A terrine is a pâté cooked with pork.

2 tbs. butter
1 medium onion, minced
3/4 lb. lean ground pork
3/4 lb. pork sausage
2 large eggs, beaten
3 cloves garlic, minced
2 tbs. flour

1/4 cup brandy
1 tsp. salt
1/2 tsp. ground allspice
1/2 tsp. dried rosemary
1/2 tsp. pepper
6 slices bacon

Heat oven to 350°. In a skillet over medium-high heat, melt butter and sauté onion until soft. Set aside to cool. In a large bowl, combine pork, sausage, eggs, garlic, flour, brandy, salt, allspice, rosemary and pepper. Stir in cooled onions. Line a 9 x 5-inch loaf pan with bacon slices. Fill with meat mixture and fold bacon over the top. Cover with foil. Place loaf pan in a large pan. Pour boiling water in large pan to halfway up loaf pan. Bake for 1 1/4 to 1 1/2 hours, or until juices are clear. Drain the fat and juices from the pan. Place a heavy weight, such as a brick wrapped in foil, on the terrine and refrigerate for several hours before serving.

CRAB MUSHROOM BAKES

This makes an elegant first course. As an alternative, the mushrooms can be coarsely diced, the appetizer baked in a large dish and served as a dip with vegetables or whole-grain breads.

¼ cup (½ stick) butter
3 large sweet onions, thinly sliced
16 large fresh mushrooms
4 oz. crabmeat
1 green onion, finely chopped
3 oz. cream cheese, softened
salt and pepper to taste
4 oz. Monterey Jack or Gruyère cheese, shredded

Heat oven to 350°. Melt butter in a large skillet and sauté onions over medium heat until golden. Divide the cooked onions among 8 ramekins or custard cups. Remove stems from mushrooms and discard. Place two mushroom caps in each dish, gill sides up. In a small bowl, combine crab, green onion, cream cheese, salt and pepper. Fill mushroom caps with this mixture. Bake for 8 minutes or until mushrooms are soft, sprinkle with cheese and continue baking 5 to 7 minutes longer until cheese melts. Serve immediately.

TOASTED PECAN SHRIMP DIP

Beer gives this dish its unique flavor. Serve with whole-grain crackers or crudités. This recipe can also work as a sandwich spread.

8 oz. cream cheese, softened
2 tbs. finely minced celery
2 tsp. grated onion
2 tbs. beer
1/4 tsp. Worcestershire sauce
1/8 tsp. dry mustard
1/2 cup cooked chopped shrimp
1/2 cup chopped toasted pecans

In a medium bowl, combine cream cheese, celery, onion, beer, Worcestershire sauce and mustard until well mixed. Stir in shrimp and pecans. Taste and adjust seasonings. Place in serving dish, cover and refrigerate several hours before serving.

SALADS

27   Feta Salad
28   Cucumber Salad
29   Orange and Onion Salad
30   Tomato Salad on Eggplant
31   Roasted Beet Salad
32   Sesame Daikon Salad
33   Raspberry Gorgonzola Salad
34   Artichokes With Crabmeat Salad
35   Melon And Cucumber Salad
36   Curry Coleslaw
37   Broccoli and Beef Salad
38   Blue Cheese and Pear Salad
39   Walnut Vinaigrette
40   Duck Salad With Curried Vinaigrette

FETA SALAD

The combination of kalamata olives and feta cheese is always a delightful change to the boring lettuce and tomato salad. It is important to use sweet onions to balance out flavors.

4 plum tomatoes
1 English cucumber, peeled
1 medium-sized sweet onion (such as Vidalia or Walla Walla)
1 large green or yellow bell pepper
10 oz. feta cheese, coarsely chopped
$1/2$ cup pitted kalamata olives

$1/4$ cup olive oil
2 tbs. fresh lemon juice or white wine vinegar
$1/2$ tsp. dried oregano
salt to taste
white pepper to taste
1 tsp. minced fresh mint

Core tomatoes and chop into large chunks. Chop cucumbers into large chunks. Cut the onions in half, then slice thinly. Thinly slice bell pepper. Add tomatoes, cucumbers, onions and pepper strips to a large bowl along with feta cheese and olives. In a small bowl, combine olive oil, lemon juice, oregano, salt and pepper. Pour dressing over the salad and gently toss to combine. Divide the salad onto four plates and sprinkle with mint. Serve immediately.

CUCUMBER SALAD

I generally prefer English cucumbers because you do not have to worry about the seeds and they are "burpless." Jalapeños are optional—substitute bell pepper if you don't want the heat.

3 English cucumbers, peeled and sliced
1 medium red onion, thinly sliced
2 red jalapeño peppers, thinly sliced
$1/4$ cup rice vinegar
2 tbs. honey, Splenda or brown sugar
$1/2$ cup warm water
$1/4$ cup chopped fresh cilantro

Arrange cucumbers, onions and jalapeños on salad plates. In a small bowl, whisk together vinegar, honey and water. Pour dressing over the vegetables and sprinkle with cilantro.

ORANGE AND ONION SALAD

It is important to use a good olive oil to enhance the simple flavors of this salad. Chicory can be substituted for the butter lettuce, and feta cheese can be added for a new twist to this recipe.

2 large oranges, peeled
1 head butter lettuce, torn
2 heads Belgian endive, thinly sliced
$\frac{1}{2}$ small red onion, thinly sliced
$\frac{1}{3}$ cup pitted black olives
1 tbs. extra-virgin olive oil
$\frac{1}{4}$ tsp. salt
$\frac{1}{8}$ tsp. pepper

Remove the white pith from oranges with a sharp knife. Holding an orange over a bowl to catch the juice, slide the knife down one side of a membrane and twist to release the segment. After removing the segments, squeeze remaining membrane to release the juice. Repeat with second orange. Place the orange segments in a bowl with the lettuce, endive, onion and olives. Whisk oil, salt and pepper into reserved orange juice and drizzle over salad, tossing to combine. Serve immediately.

TOMATO SALAD ON EGGPLANT

A simple tomato salad is served on a broiled eggplant round. This is unique and nutritious.

2 small eggplants
3 tbs. olive oil, divided
salt and pepper to taste
3 tomatoes, chopped
1 small red onion, chopped
3 tbs. finely sliced fresh basil
1 tbs. capers
2–3 tsp. balsamic vinegar
1 tbs. olive oil

Heat broiler. Slice the eggplants into $\frac{1}{2}$-inch rounds. Brush both sides with 2 tbs. of the oil, sprinkle with salt and pepper and broil until browned and tender. Cool eggplant to room temperature. In a bowl, gently combine tomatoes, onion, basil, capers, vinegar, remaining 1 tbs. olive oil, salt and pepper. Taste and adjust seasonings. Serve by spooning tomato mixture over broiled eggplant rounds.

ROASTED BEET SALAD

Roasting beets is easy to do and brings out their natural sweetness. Consider serving with small bread rounds or vegetables. This salad makes a colorful entree for lunch.

1½ lbs. fresh beets
1 tsp. olive oil
3 cloves garlic, minced
¼ tsp. salt
2 tsp. fresh lemon juice
2 tbs. extra-virgin olive oil

½ head lettuce of choice (butter lettuce or
   green leaf)
½ head slivered radicchio
½ cup crumbled feta cheese
½ cup pitted kalamata olives

Heat oven to 350. Leave the skin on the beets, wash thoroughly, coat with olive oil and wrap in foil. Cook 45 to 60 minutes or until a fork easily pierces the flesh. Remove beets from oven and, using a towel, rub the skins off. Cut beets into chunks and cool to room temperature. In a bowl, stir garlic, salt, lemon juice and oil together. Divide lettuce, radicchio and beets onto salad plates. Sprinkle with feta cheese and olives. Pour on dressing and serve immediately.

SESAME DAIKON SALAD

The nutty flavor of toasted sesame seeds adds a special dimension to this salad. It is important to drain the radishes; otherwise the salad will be watery.

2 medium daikon radishes, peeled
4 medium carrots, grated
2 tbs. rice vinegar
4 tsp. sweet mirin (rice wine)
1/4 cup soy sauce
2 tsp. toasted sesame oil
3 tbs. toasted sesame seeds

Grate daikon radishes and place in a colander to drain for 5 minutes. Squeeze out any excess moisture and place in a bowl. Add carrots and stir to combine. In a small bowl, whisk together vinegar, mirin, soy sauce and sesame oil. Taste and adjust seasoning. Stir dressing into the shredded vegetables and sprinkle with sesame seeds.

RASPBERRY GORGONZOLA SALAD

If raspberries are out of season, dried cranberries (or Craisins) can be substituted. Don't restrict yourself to just these greens—allow yourself to experiment with new flavors and textures.

1 head butter lettuce
½ head endive, finely chopped
½ head radicchio or red cabbage, cut into slivers
1–2 tbs. butter
½ cup pecans

1 pint fresh raspberries
¼ cup crumbled Gorgonzola cheese
¼ cup extra-virgin olive oil
3–4 tbs. balsamic vinegar
2 tsp. Dijon mustard
1 pinch salt

Tear lettuce into bite-sized pieces. Place lettuce in a large bowl with endive and radicchio. In a skillet, melt butter and toast pecans over medium-high heat, stirring frequently, until browned. Gently toss raspberries, Gorgonzola and pecans with the greens. In a small bowl, whisk olive oil, vinegar, mustard and salt together. Taste and adjust seasonings. Pour enough of the dressing over salad to coat lightly and serve immediately.

ARTICHOKES WITH CRABMEAT SALAD

This is a fancy way to serve salad and worth the extra effort. If possible, reserve 6 large pieces of crabmeat as a garnish.

6 small fresh artichokes
juice of 2 lemons
1/3 cup sour cream
1/3 cup mayonnaise

1 tsp. mild curry powder (or to taste)
salt and pepper to taste
3/4 lb. crabmeat
lemon slices, for garnish

Using a serrated knife, cut 1/3 from the top and a small portion from base of each artichoke. With scissors, clip tips of remaining leaves. Bring salted water to a boil in a large pot and add lemon juice. Put artichokes in pot and weight them down to keep below water line. Cook 25 to 30 minutes until soft, drain upside down and cool to room temperature. With a spoon, scoop out center choke and discard. Refrigerate artichokes.

In a small bowl, combine sour cream, mayonnaise, curry, salt, pepper and crabmeat. Taste and adjust seasonings. Fill cavity of artichokes with salad until brimming over the top. Garnish each artichoke with a slice of lemon.

MELON AND CUCUMBER SALAD

This very refreshing salad is both colorful and flavorful. Mint is the surprising ingredient. Only fresh mint can be used in this recipe.

1 ripe honeydew melon
1 English cucumber, peeled and sliced
1 lb. plum tomatoes
2 tbs. balsamic vinegar
6 tbs. olive or vegetable oil
1 tbs. chopped fresh parsley

2 tsp. chopped fresh chives
1 tbs. chopped fresh mint
1 tbs. sugar
1 tsp. salt
$\frac{1}{2}$ tsp. white pepper

Remove seeds from honeydew, cut into balls with a melon baller and place in a large serving bowl along with cucumber. Peel tomatoes, remove seeds, chop coarsely and add to bowl. In a food processor workbowl or blender container, place vinegar, oil, parsley, chives, mint, sugar, salt and pepper. Pulse to combine. Taste and adjust seasonings. Pour dressing over salad, toss, and refrigerate before serving.

CURRY COLESLAW

Cabbage has a tendency to absorb dressing. For that reason, I always reserve some dressing to add just before serving. Use a mild (not hot) curry in this recipe.

1 small head cabbage, coarsely chopped
1 carrot, coarsely chopped
$1/2$ cup mayonnaise
$1/4$ cup rice vinegar
1 tbs. fresh lemon juice
1 tsp. curry powder (or more to taste)
1–2 tbs. sugar
salt and pepper to taste

Place cabbage and carrot in food processor workbowl and process until grated. Place in a large bowl. In a small bowl, combine mayonnaise, vinegar, lemon juice, curry powder, sugar, salt and pepper. Taste and adjust seasonings. Stir about $2/3$ of the dressing into grated vegetables and refrigerate until ready to serve. Just before serving, stir in the remaining dressing.

BROCCOLI AND BEEF SALAD

This high-protein salad can be varied by using different types of meat. Pork cutlet strips or even cooked chicken tenders can be substituted for the steak.

1½ lbs. broccoli
½ cup sesame oil, divided
6–8 fresh mushrooms, quartered
¼ cup balsamic vinegar
¼ cup soy sauce
2 cloves garlic, minced

½–1 tsp. sugar
1 lb. boneless strip sirloin steak
1 can (14 oz.) artichoke hearts, drained and
   quartered
2 ripe avocados, coarsely chopped
2 tbs. toasted sesame seeds

Peel broccoli stems, cut into thin slices and cut tops into small florets. In a skillet or wok, heat ¼ cup of the oil over medium-high heat and sauté stems for 2 minutes. Add florets and continue to stir-fry about 4 minutes, until broccoli is crisp-tender. Transfer to a serving bowl. Heat remaining ¼ cup oil in skillet, stir-fry mushrooms for 4 minutes and add to bowl with broccoli. In a small bowl, whisk together vinegar, soy sauce, garlic and sugar. Pour dressing over vegetables.

Sauté steak to medium-rare (or desired doneness) then cut into thin strips. Add steak strips and artichoke hearts to broccoli mixture and stir to combine. Refrigerate for several hours before serving. Add avocado and sesame seeds just before serving.

BLUE CHEESE AND PEAR SALAD

Blue cheese and pears make a good marriage of flavors. Try to find pears that are ripe and flavorful. Toasting the walnuts is important to the taste of this salad.

$1/2$ cup coarsely chopped walnuts
6 oz. blue cheese
$1/4$ cup heavy cream
4 firm pears

1 lemon, halved
4 cups watercress sprigs or greens of choice
3–4 tbs. *Walnut Vinaigrette,* page 39
pepper to taste

Heat oven to 350°. Spread walnuts on a cookie sheet, place in oven and toast nuts until lightly browned, 3 to 5 minutes. In a small bowl, coarsely mash blue cheese with a fork, add cream and gently stir until just combined. Peel pears and rub with lemon half to prevent discoloration. Cut each pear into quarters and remove core. Cut quarters lengthwise into $1/4$-inch-thick slices and sprinkle with lemon juice. Toss watercress with *Walnut Vinaigrette* and arrange on four individual serving plates. Place a dollop of blue cheese mixture on each pear slice and arrange the slices around watercress in spiral pattern. Sprinkle with chopped walnuts and season with pepper.

WALNUT VINAIGRETTE

This dressing can be used on most green salads, and goes especially well with any fruit and lettuce combinations.

2 tbs. balsamic vinegar
1 tsp. Dijon mustard
$1/4$ cup walnut oil
1 tbs. safflower oil
salt and pepper to taste

Combine vinegar and mustard in a small bowl and whisk well. Slowly drizzle in oils, whisking constantly until smooth. Season with salt and pepper.

DUCK SALAD WITH CURRIED VINAIGRETTE

Duck is not as scary to cook as most people think. Piercing the skin allows the fat to be released during the roasting process. I especially like to use raspberry vinegar and fresh raspberries in this recipe when they are available.

1 duck, about 4½ lb.
1 cup olive or vegetable oil
¼ cup balsamic vinegar or raspberry vinegar
⅓ cup honey
1 tsp. curry powder
salt and pepper to taste
8 stalks fresh asparagus
1 cup snow peas
1 head butter lettuce, washed and torn
2 cups sliced fresh pineapple
1 cup whole blanched almonds, toasted
½ cup fresh raspberries, optional

Heat oven to 325°. Rinse and dry duck, them trim off excess skin. Prick duck all over with a fork. Line a roasting pan with foil. Place duck in pan and roast for I hour or until cooked through. Remove from oven and cool completely. Remove meat from the bone and cut into bite-sized pieces. Set aside. In a food processor workbowl or blender container, combine oil, vinegar, honey, curry powder, salt and pepper. Taste and adjust seasonings. One hour before serving, combine duck meat with a bit of the dressing to coat.

Remove woody ends from asparagus and discard. Blanch asparagus and snow peas in boiling water for $1/2$ to 1 minute. Plunge in ice water to stop cooking. Dry and slice asparagus and snow peas diagonally. In a large bowl, gently toss lettuce, asparagus, snow peas, pineapple, almonds and reserved duck meat. Drizzle with vinaigrette just before serving. If desired, sprinkle with fresh raspberries.

SOUPS

CARROT AND SHALLOT SOUP

Carrots are higher in carbohydrates, so serve this as a starter course, not a main dish. Include a large tossed salad and a good protein entrée to accompany this soup.

3 tbs. butter
4–5 large shallots, minced, or 1/2 cup minced onion
6 cups chopped carrots
1 1/2–2 qts. chicken broth
salt and white pepper to taste
1/2 cup heavy cream
1 tbs. minced fresh dill, or 1 tsp. dried
heavy cream, for garnish

Heat butter in a stockpot over medium heat and sauté shallots until tender. Add carrots and cook for 10 minutes longer. Add enough broth to cover, bring to a simmer, and cook until carrots are tender. Puree soup in a blender container and return to heat (do not boil). Add salt, white pepper, cream and dill; taste and adjust seasonings. Serve with a dollop of cream on top.

SEAFOOD SOUP

This hearty soup is loaded with fish and vegetables. Even though there are a lot of ingredients, this recipe goes together quickly. Serve with a crisp tossed salad.

1 tbs. olive oil
1/4 lb. bacon, diced
1 medium onion, chopped
1 leek, washed and finely chopped
3 cloves garlic, minced
1 stalk celery, chopped
1/2 green pepper, finely chopped
1 cup dry white wine
1 can (12 oz.) plum tomatoes, chopped
1 can (8 oz.) tomato sauce

1 tsp. dried oregano
1 tsp. dried basil
3 tbs. chopped fresh parsley
salt and pepper to taste
1/2 lb. squid, cleaned and sliced into rounds
3/4 cup clam juice
1 can (7 1/2 oz.) whole baby clams
1/2 lb. prawns, cleaned and peeled
1/2 lb. red snapper, cut into cubes
1/2 lb. cod, cut into cubes

Heat oil in a stockpot over medium heat and cook bacon until crisp. Add onion, leek, garlic, celery and green pepper, and cook until vegetables are soft. Add wine and cook 1 minute longer. Add tomatoes, tomato sauce, oregano, basil, parsley, salt and pepper. Cook for 15 minutes. Add squid and clam juice, reduce heat to low and gently simmer for 45 minutes. Add clams, prawns, snapper and cod. Cook for 5 to 6 minutes, or until fish is just cooked and prawns are pink.

THREE-ONION SOUP

Caramelizing onions brings out their natural sweetness. Using a variety of onions adds dimension to the taste and texture. The toasted bread rounds are optional.

2 tbs. olive oil
2 tbs. butter
3 medium yellow onions, thinly sliced
1 medium red onions, peeled and thinly
   sliced
2 large shallots, sliced

1/4 cup dry sherry or cognac
4 cups beef or vegetable broth
1 1/4 tsp. salt (or to taste)
pepper to taste
8 slices French bread, toasted
1 cup shredded Gruyère cheese

Heat oil and butter over medium-low heat in a stockpot. Add yellow onions, red onions and shallots and cook for 45 minutes, stirring occasionally, until onions turn brown (caramelize). Stir in sherry and add broth. Increase the heat to high, bring to a boil, then reduce heat to low and simmer for 20 minutes, partially covered. Season with salt and pepper to taste.

Heat oven to 450°. Pour soup into ovenproof bowls, top with toasted bread and sprinkle with cheese. Bake about 10 minutes until cheese melts.

CREAM OF CUCUMBER SOUP

This refreshing chilled soup would go well with hearty, whole-grain bread.

3 medium cucumbers
1 medium onion, chopped
1 cup chicken broth
2 tbs. flour
$1/2$ tsp. salt
$1/4$ tsp. white pepper
1 pinch garlic powder
1 cup sour cream
cucumber slices, for garnish
fresh dill weed, for garnish

Peel, seed and chop cucumbers. In a blender container or food processor workbowl, puree cucumbers, onion, broth, flour, salt, pepper, and garlic powder. Pour into a bowl, add sour cream, taste and adjust seasonings. Refrigerate until cold. When serving, place a slice of cucumber on top of the soup and sprinkle with dill.

CREAM OF WATERCRESS SOUP

Watercress has a fresh, "green" flavor. This recipe works well as a first course dish.

3 cups milk
2 thin slices onion
2 bay leaves
12 peppercorns
5 tbs. butter, divided

3 tbs. flour
salt and white pepper to taste
1 lb. watercress, cleaned
1/3 cup chicken broth
1/3 cup heavy cream

Place milk in a heavy saucepan and heat to just below boiling. Remove milk from heat and add onion, bay leaves and peppercorns and set aside to steep for 10 minutes. In a separate pan, melt 3 tbs. of the butter, stir in flour and cook over medium heat for 2 minutes. Strain the milk mixture and whisk into the flour/butter mixture over medium-high heat until mixture thickens.

Set aside a few sprigs of watercress for garnish. Cook the remaining watercress in a large pot of boiling salted water for 1 minute. Drain watercress, squeeze dry and chop. Melt remaining 2 tbs. butter in a stockpot, add watercress and sauté for several minutes. Stir in milk mixture and simmer soup for 10 minutes longer. Puree soup in food processor workbowl or blender container. Pour soup back into stockpot, add chicken broth and bring to a boil. Reduce heat to medium and stir in cream. Serve with a sprig of watercress for garnish.

LENTIL SOUP WITH SAUSAGE

Lentils are high in protein and very versatile. The addition of kielbasa gives heartiness to the soup and lots of flavor. Adding a sprinkling of cilantro will give the lentils a clean, crisp flavor.

3 cups beef broth
1½ cups dried lentils
1 large onion, chopped
3 cloves garlic, minced
1 carrot, diced
2 ribs celery, diced
1 tbs. soy sauce

1 tsp. oyster sauce
½ lb. Polish kielbasa (or other cooked
 sausages)
1 tbs. vinegar
salt and pepper to taste
minced fresh cilantro or parsley, for garnish

In a stockpot, bring broth to a boil and slowly stir in lentils. Add onion, garlic, carrot,, celery, soy sauce and oyster sauce. Cook about 25 minutes or until lentils are soft. Cut sausage into small bite-sized pieces and stir into lentils. Cook for 5 minutes. Add vinegar, salt and pepper to taste. Serve with a sprinkling of cilantro for garnish.

ARTICHOKE AND CRAB SOUP

This simple but elegant soup is easy to prepare. For a gourmet garnish, float a whole piece of crab leg in the center with a lemon slice and a few chopped chives.

6 oz. snow crabmeat
1 can (8½ oz.) water-packed artichoke hearts, drained
1½ cups chicken broth
¼ tsp. dried oregano
½ tsp. salt
1 pinch white pepper
2 tbs. lemon juice
1 cup heavy cream
thin lemon slices, for garnish
chopped fresh chives, for garnish

Drain any excess liquid from crabmeat. Set crabmeat aside. In a food processor workbowl or blender container, puree artichoke hearts with broth, oregano, salt and pepper. Pour into a saucepan and heat slowly over low heat. Adjust seasonings, then add cream and crabmeat. Refrigerate soup until cold. Garnish with lemon slices and chives.

SAUTÉED BEEF AND MUSHROOM SOUP

Servings: 4

This soup is high in protein and can be served as a main dish. Serve with colorful steamed vegetables and a hearty whole-grain bread.

1¼ lb. top round steak
¼ cup (½ stick) butter, divided
1 tbs. olive oil
5 oz. red wine or port
2 tbs. flour
1 can (10 oz.) beef broth
1 bay leaf
2 sprigs fresh thyme
3 fresh parsley sprigs
½ lb. sliced fresh mushrooms
3 cloves garlic, minced
2 tbs. minced fresh parsley

Heat oven to 200°. Cut the meat into 4 or 5 strips. Heat 2 tbs. of the butter over medium-high heat in a stockpot and add the oil. Brown the meat on all sides. Place in a pan in the oven to keep warm. Add wine to the pot. Cook, stirring, until reduced by half. Pour wine over the meat.

In the same pot, melt the remaining 2 tbs. butter, add the flour and cook until straw-colored. Add the broth and cook, stirring, until it boils. Add the reserved meat and wine. Place bay leaf, thyme and parsley sprigs in cheesecloth and tie with a string (this is known as a bouquet garni). Add this to the pot and simmer gently for 45 minutes.

Remove stems from the mushrooms and discard. Add the mushrooms and garlic to the pot with the garlic. Cook for 20 minutes longer or until the meat is tender and the mushrooms are cooked. Remove and discard the bouquet garni. Break up the meat into bite-sized pieces and divide among serving bowls. Lay mushrooms over the top of the meat; strain the sauce over the mushrooms and sprinkle parsley on top for garnish. Serve immediately.

FAST TOMATO SOUP

This soup can be served hot or chilled. For best results, try to obtain tomatoes that actually have flavor, such as plum tomatoes that hopefully have been ripened on the vine.

3 green onions, cut into 1-inch pieces
1 tsp. lemon zest
6 large tomatoes
$1/2$–1 tsp. honey
salt and pepper to taste
$1/4$ tsp. dried marjoram

$1/2$ tsp. dried thyme
2 tbs. fresh lemon juice
1 cup chicken broth
$1/2$ cup sour cream, for garnish
1 tbs. minced fresh parsley, for garnish

Place green onions and lemon zest in blender container or food processor workbowl and process until finely minced. Cut tomatoes in half. Gently squeeze the halves to remove the seeds. Add the tomatoes to the processor and pulse until finely chopped. Transfer tomato mixture to a saucepan and add honey, salt, pepper, marjoram, thyme, lemon juice and broth. Cook for 10 minutes over medium heat, then return mixture to food processor workbowl and puree until smooth. Strain soup through a sieve before serving. Serve either hot or chilled. Mix sour cream with parsley and spoon a dollop of this mixture in the center of the soup.

LEEK SOUP

The leek is a forgotten vegetable. It has a wonderful flavor and is easy to work with. Keep in mind that leeks must be washed very carefully, rinsing between each layer.

3 tbs. butter
5 large leeks
1 clove garlic, minced
4 cups beef broth
salt and pepper to taste
2 cups shredded Parmesan cheese

Cut tough leaves off top of leeks and discard. Cut leeks in half and rinse well to remove sand. Thinly slice leeks. Melt butter in heavy 2-quart saucepan over low heat. Sauté leeks until soft. Add garlic, broth, salt and pepper. Simmer until leeks are very tender. Serve hot with a sprinkling of Parmesan cheese for garnish.

GREAT NORTHERN BEAN SOUP

Servings: 8

This was one of my mother's favorite recipes. During the Depression, bean soup was survival food and was associated with good times with her cousins. For a heartier soup, try adding a ham hock for flavor and texture

2 cups dried great Northern beans
1 tbs. olive oil
2 tbs. butter
1 large onion, chopped
1 cup cleaned, chopped leeks
1 large tomato, seeded and coarsely chopped
1/2 cup chopped carrots
1/2 cup chopped celery

9 cloves garlic, chopped
6 slices bacon, diced
11 cups chicken broth
1 tsp. dried thyme
1/2 tsp. chopped dried rosemary
salt and pepper to taste
1/2–3/4 cup heavy cream

Place beans in stockpot and cover with water by 2 inches. Soak beans overnight. Drain beans, discarding soaking liquid.

Heat olive oil and butter over medium-high heat in a stockpot. Add onions and leeks and sauté for about 8 minutes until soft. Add tomato, carrots, celery, garlic and bacon and cook until vegetables are soft, about 5 minutes. Stir in soaked beans, chicken broth, thyme and rosemary. Cover and cook over low heat for 1 hour, stirring occasionally. When beans are very tender, puree soup in batches in a blender container or food processor workbowl. Return pureed soup to pot and stir in salt, pepper and cream. Taste and adjust seasonings before serving.

MULLIGATAWNY SOUP

This hearty soup originated in India. It is loaded with vegetables, apples and chicken and seasoned with curry.

3 tbs. vegetable oil
3 cloves garlic, cut in half
$\frac{1}{2}$ cup finely diced onion
$\frac{1}{2}$ cup finely diced carrots
$\frac{1}{2}$ cup finely diced celery
1 bay leaf
1 cup diced unpeeled Golden Delicious apples
$\frac{1}{4}$ cup flour
$\frac{1}{2}$ tbs. curry powder
$\frac{1}{4}$ tsp. ground cumin
5 cups chicken broth
$\frac{1}{2}$–$\frac{3}{4}$ cup rice
$\frac{3}{4}$ cup diced cooked chicken
2 tbs. chopped fresh parsley
salt and pepper to taste

In a heavy stockpot, heat oil over medium-high heat and sauté garlic until it begins to brown. Remove garlic and discard. Add onions, carrots, celery, bay leaf and apples to pot and sauté until vegetables are tender. Stir in flour, curry and cumin until vegetables are coated. Add broth and rice and simmer about 20 minutes until rice is tender. Just before serving, add chicken, parsley, salt and pepper. Taste and adjust seasonings.

VEGETABLES

TOASTED HAZELNUT ASPARAGUS

I always like to dress up vegetables with unique flavors and textures. Toasted hazelnuts are perfect, but toasted almonds also work well with this recipe.

1½ lbs. asparagus
1 tsp. grated orange zest
1 tbs. orange juice
1½ tsp. lemon juice
2 tbs. olive oil
salt and pepper to taste
3 tbs. finely chopped hazelnuts, toasted

Remove woody ends from asparagus and discard. Cook asparagus in boiling salted water for about 10 minutes. When asparagus is just barely tender, drain and place in a serving dish. Whisk orange zest, orange juice, lemon juice, olive oil, salt and pepper together in a small bowl. Taste and adjust seasonings. Pour dressing over asparagus and sprinkle with hazelnuts.

LEMONGRASS ZUCCHINI

Lemongrass has a zesty lemony flavor that enhances sauces, poultry, vegetables and soups. Only the tender white section of the stalk is used. If you are unable to find lemongrass, substitute lemon juice and/or powdered lemongrass.

1$\frac{1}{2}$ lbs. medium-sized zucchini
1 stalk fresh lemongrass
1 tsp. sugar
3 tbs. minced fresh mint
1 tsp. olive oil
2 tsp. sesame oil
1 tsp. peanut oil

Cut zucchini into $\frac{1}{2}$-inch slices. Cut off the bottom 2 to 3 inches of lemongrass stalk, and discard the rest. Peel away the tough outer layers and mince the tender white core. Place sugar on a cutting board, place mint on sugar and finely chop the mint. Combine lemongrass, sugar, mint and olive oil and pound into a paste with a mortar and pestle. In a nonstick skillet, heat sesame and peanut oils over medium-high heat and sauté until zucchini is golden. Add the lemongrass paste and sauté, stirring, until paste is well distributed.

BRAISED FENNEL

Fennel imparts a wonderful anise or licorice flavor. Fennel generally needs to be steamed before adding it as an ingredient to casseroles.

2 bulbs fennel
3–4 cloves garlic, minced
2 tbs. melted butter or olive oil
salt and pepper to taste
1/4 cup dry white wine or chicken broth
1/2 cup shredded Parmesan cheese
2 tbs. finely chopped fresh basil, or 2 tsp. dried basil

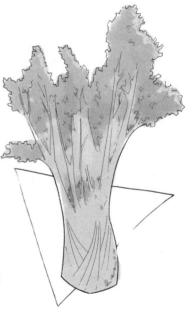

Heat oven to 325°. Grease a small baking dish; set aside. Cut the fennel bulbs into thin wedges and steam for about 10 minutes or until just tender. Arrange the steamed fennel in prepared baking dish, sprinkle with garlic and drizzle with melted butter. Season with salt and pepper, and add wine. Cover and bake for 20 minutes, remove cover and stir. Sprinkle with Parmesan and basil, and bake uncovered until browned, about 10 minutes.

ROASTED PEANUT BOK CHOY

Roasting peanuts creates a wonderful smell in your kitchen before guests arrive. Sometimes I like to add a few teaspoons of peanut butter to the sauce for extra flavor.

2 tsp. peanut oil, divided
1/4 cup whole raw peanuts
1/8 tsp. crushed red pepper flakes
1 pinch salt
1 bunch bok choy

4 cloves garlic, minced
4 tsp. minced fresh ginger
1 tsp. cornstarch
3 tbs. cold water
2 tbs. soy sauce

Heat 1 tsp. of the oil in a small skillet over medium heat and sauté peanuts until golden brown. Chop the peanuts, stir in red pepper flakes and salt. Set aside. Add the remaining 1 tsp. peanut oil to the skillet, stir in garlic and ginger and sauté for 1 minute. Cut the bok choy into 1/2-inch slices (leave the leaves whole), add to skillet and stir-fry over medium-high heat until crisp-tender and glossy. Mix cornstarch with cold water and soy sauce in a small bowl and stir into boy choy. Stir-fry for 1 to 2 minutes until sauce is thickened. Sprinkle on reserved peanut mixture and serve immediately.

CABBAGE WITH PANCETTA AND ONIONS

Servings: 4

Pancetta is an Italian bacon. It you cannot obtain pancetta, use thick-sliced bacon instead. I prefer to use savoy cabbage, but green cabbage will also work well. Goat cheese can also be substituted for the Parmesan cheese.

1 head savoy cabbage, cut into thin strips
2 tbs. olive oil
4 oz. diced pancetta
1 large onion, chopped
1 cup vegetable or chicken broth
salt and pepper to taste
1/4 cup shredded Parmesan cheese

In a saucepan, steam cabbage over high heat for 5 minutes or until tender. Heat oil in a large skillet, add pancetta and onion and cook over medium heat until pancetta is crisp, 5 to 6 minutes. Stir in cabbage and cook for about 10 minutes or until cabbage is lightly browned. Add broth and cook 4 minutes longer. Season with salt and pepper to taste. Serve immediately with a sprinkling of Parmesan cheese on top.

LEEK AND WILD RICE GRATIN

Servings: 4

Wild rice is not rice at all but actually a grass. Celery root, or celeriac, is a vegetable that looks a bit like a knobby potato and has an intense celery flavor.

1 cup wild rice
½ tsp. salt
2 large leeks
¼ cup (½ stick) butter, divided
¼ cup chopped onions
2 tbs. flour
1½ cups milk
1 celery root, peeled and grated
2 tbs. lemon juice
3 tbs. minced fresh parsley
salt and pepper to taste
½ cup shredded Gruyère cheese
⅓ cup shredded Parmesan cheese

In a saucepan over high heat, bring a quart of water to a boil. Add wild rice and salt to boiling water, reduce heat to medium, cover and cook for 45 minutes. Drain and set aside.

While rice is cooking, trim tough green tops from leeks. and discard Split leeks in half lengthwise, rinse well to remove sand and slice 1/2-inch thick. Melt 3 tbs. of the butter in a skillet over medium heat, add leeks and onions and cook for 3 to 4 minutes. Stir in flour and cook 2 minutes longer. In a small saucepan, heat the milk to just below the boiling point. Add to onion mixture and cook, stirring constantly, until sauce thickens.

Heat oven to 400°. Lightly butter a 9 x 13-inch baking dish. Melt remaining 1 tbs. butter in a skillet over medium heat. Add celery root, lemon juice and parsley and cook for about 5 minutes or until celery root is tender. Season with salt and pepper. In a large bowl, stir together rice, leeks, onions, celery root, sauce, and cheese. Transfer to prepared baking dish and bake for 20 to 25 minutes or until lightly browned and heated through.

GREEN BEANS WITH GARLIC AIOLI

Aioli—a garlicky mayonnaise—works well with most steamed vegetables. This recipe for aioli will make more than is necessary for this dish. Refrigerate the leftover sauce. Raw eggs can cause salmonella; use Egg Beaters instead if you're concerned.

1 large egg, or $1/4$ cup Egg Beaters
1 pinch salt
3 tbs. fresh lemon juice
3 cloves garlic, minced

$1/4$ cup extra-virgin olive oil
$3/4$ cup light olive oil
2 lbs. green beans
minced fresh parsley, optional

Place egg, salt , lemon juice and garlic in a blender container or food processor workbowl and blend on high until well combined. Add extra-virgin olive oil and blend until mixture turns light yellow. With the machine running, slowly drizzle light olive oil in a steady stream until all the oil is incorporated and aioli is thick. Taste and add more salt, garlic or lemon juice of you wish. Refrigerate until ready to use.

Tip and tail the beans, then steam in a saucepan over high heat until tender, 3 to 5 minutes. Toss the beans with some of the aioli and serve warm. Sprinkle a little minced parsley on top for garnish, if desired.

SAUTEED CHERRY TOMATOES

Servings: 4–6

Cherry tomatoes are generally served raw. This accompaniment to a meal is quick to fix and adds beautiful color to the plate. Experiment with spices like cumin for Mexican meals, or oregano for Italian, or even ginger and garlic.

3 tbs. olive oil
3 tbs. butter
2 quarts cherry tomatoes, stemmed
1 tsp. sugar
1/2 tsp. salt
1 tsp. Tabasco sauce, optional
2 tbs. minced fresh basil or parsley, optional

In a large skillet, heat oil and butter over high heat. Add tomatoes, sugar, salt and Tabasco and toss in pan, shaking back and forth, for 2 to 3 minutes. Do not overcook, or skins will split. Remove from the heat and sprinkle with additional salt, if desired. Garnish with basil.

ONION JAM

Onion jam is a "mass" of caramelized onions that can be served with beef, pork and poultry. It can also be used as a side dish or simply a spread on toasted bread rounds as an appetizer.

4 large onions (preferably a sweet onion such as Walla Walla)
2 tbs. butter
1 tsp. vegetable oil
1 tsp. salt
2 tbs. brown sugar

Thinly slice onions. Melt butter and oil in a heavy skillet (preferably cast iron) over medium-high heat, add onions and sauté for 8 to 10 minutes. Reduce heat to medium, add salt and partially cover pan. Continue cooking, stirring frequently, until onions are very soft and caramel-colored, about 30 minutes. Stir in brown sugar until dissolved and serve immediately, or refrigerate until ready to use.

ROASTED EGGPLANT WITH TOMATOES

This is a great side dish for a lamb or beef entrée. The ingredients are simple, but the roasting takes a bit of time.

2¼ lbs. eggplants, peeled
7 tbs. extra-virgin olive oil, divided
salt and pepper to taste
1½ lbs. plum tomatoes, quartered

1½ cups chopped onions
4 large garlic cloves, minced
½ cup chopped fresh basil
2 tbs. balsamic vinegar

Heat oven to 400°. Coarsely chop eggplant, toss in a bowl with ¼ cup of the olive oil and season with salt and pepper. Spread on a cookie sheet and roast for 75 minutes, stirring every 20 minutes, until eggplant is softened and starting to brown. Set aside. Keep oven at 400°.

Toss tomatoes with 2 tbs. of the oil and season with salt and pepper. Spread on cookie sheet and roast for 1 hour.

Heat remaining 1 tbs. oil in a heavy skillet over medium heat. Add onions and garlic and sauté for about 15 minutes, until onions are translucent. Coarsely chop tomatoes. Place in a large bowl along with onion mixture and roasted eggplant. Stir in basil, vinegar, salt and pepper.

CURRIED GREENS

The beauty of this recipe is that you can use countless combinations of greens for variety. Instead of the spinach and mustard, try an equal quantity of Swiss chard, red chard, dandelion greens, kale, etc.

1 large onion, cut into thin wedges
6 tbs. olive oil, divided
salt to taste
2/3 cup chopped salted cashews
2 tsp. curry powder (or to taste)
1 tsp. ground cumin
1 tsp. mustard seeds
1 tsp. ground coriander
1/2 tsp. cinnamon
1/4 tsp. cayenne pepper
1 1/2 lb. fresh spinach, washed, stems removed
1 lb. mustard greens, washed, stems removed
1/2 cup water

In a heavy skillet over medium heat, sauté onions in 3 tbs. of the olive oil and sprinkle with salt. Cook until golden brown, 15 to 20 minutes. Add cashews to onions and cook until nuts are lightly toasted. In a small bowl, combine curry, cumin, mustard seeds, coriander, cinnamon and cayenne. Stir 1½ tsp. of spice mixture into onion mixture and sauté for 1 minute, then remove from heat and set aside.

Heat remaining 3 tbs. oil in a large pot over medium-high heat until hot but not smoking. Add remaining spice mixture and cook for 30 seconds. Immediately stir in greens and water and cook, stirring, until liquid is evaporated and the greens are tender, about 3 to 5 minutes. Sprinkle greens with reserved onions. Serve immediately.

ROOT VEGETABLE JULIENNE

"Julienne" simply means cut into thin or matchstick strips. This dish is great for dinner parties since the vegetables can be prepared well ahead of time and cooked the last minute. Parsnips can be substituted for turnips if desired.

2 carrots, peeled
2 stalks celery
1 turnip, peeled
1 medium onion

1 bunch broccoli
3 tbs. butter
salt and pepper taste

Cut carrots, celery, and turnips into julienne (matchstick) strips. Cut onion into quarters and then cut each quarter into slivers, separating the layers. Peel broccoli stems and cut into julienne strips. Leave florets in large clumps. Bring a pot of water to a boil, add broccoli florets and cook until crisp-tender. Rinse in cold water to revive the color. Cut florets into small pieces and set aside. Melt 2 tbs. of the butter in a skillet over medium-high heat, add broccoli stems, carrots, celery, turnips and onion and sauté for 1 minute. Cover, reduce heat to low and cook until the vegetables are tender. Melt the remaining 1 tbs. butter in a separate skillet over medium heat, add the broccoli florets and sauté, stir ring, until heated through. Season with salt and pepper. Pour broccoli into serving dish and cover with root vegetables.

GOURMET BROCCOLI

In a pinch, you can use two 10-ounce packages frozen chopped broccoli. Cook according to package directions and drain well.

1½ lbs. fresh broccoli
2 tbs. butter
2 tbs. flour
2½ tsp. chicken-seasoned broth base
¼ tsp. salt (or to taste)
1 cup hot milk

3 tbs. melted butter
⅓ cup hot water
1 cup herbed-seasoned stuffing mix
⅓ cup coarsely chopped toasted almonds or walnuts

Heat oven to 400°. In a saucepan over high heat, cook broccoli in boiling salted water until crisp-tender. Drain and chop coarsely. In a small saucepan over medium heat, melt butter and whisk in flour. Cook, stirring, for 1 minute. Add broth base, salt and milk and cook, stirring, until thickened. In a medium bowl, stir together melted butter, hot water and stuffing mix until combined. Stir in nuts.

Place cooked broccoli in a greased 1-quart casserole dish, pour white sauce over the broccoli and top with stuffing mixture. Press the stuffing down and bake uncovered for 20 minutes. Serve immediately.

EGGS

GORGONZOLA FRITTATA

This breakfast recipe is loaded with vegetables and lots of flavor. Serve with thick sliced bacon or country sausage.

2 tbs. olive oil
1 yellow onion, diced
3 cloves garlic, minced
1/2 fennel bulb, thinly sliced
1 cup broccoli florets
1 large red tomato, seeded and diced

6 eggs
salt and pepper to taste
1/2 cup crumbled Gorgonzola cheese
1/4 cup pitted chopped kalamata olives
2 tbs. toasted pine nuts

Heat broiler. Heat oil over medium heat in a large cast iron skillet (or a pan that is ovenproof). Add onion, garlic and fennel and cook for 7 to 10 minutes until vegetables are well browned. Add broccoli and cook for 3 minutes longer. Sprinkle with tomatoes and press vegetables down in the pan to help form the frittata. In a bowl, beat eggs with salt and pepper. Pour eggs over vegetables in skillet and cook over medium heat for about 2 minutes. Sprinkle with Gorgonzola, olives and pine nuts. Place the skillet under a broiler and cook for 2 to 5 minutes, until eggs are set. Serve immediately.

LAYERED EGG AND VEGETABLE CASSEROLE

This versatile layered dish of fresh vegetables, cheese and eggs can be served as breakfast, brunch, lunch or even dinner. I prefer to use Parmigiano-Reggiano for the cheese.

$1/4$ cup olive oil, divided
4 cups finely chopped leeks
$1 1/2$ cup sliced celery
6–7 cups Swiss chard, coarsely chopped
4 eggs
$2/3$ cup shredded Parmesan cheese
1 cup heavy cream
$3/4$ cup ricotta cheese
$1/2$ tsp. cayenne pepper
1 tbs. olive oil
salt and pepper to taste

Heat oven to 350°. Oil a 2-quart casserole and set aside. Heat 1 tbs. of the olive oil in a large skillet over medium heat, add leeks and cook until leeks are tender. Set leeks aside in a large bowl. Add 1 tbs. of the oil to skillet with the celery and sauté until tender. Add celery to leeks in bowl. Add 1 tbs. of the oil to skillet and sauté Swiss chard 2 minutes. Add Swiss chard to leeks in bowl.

In a small bowl, whisk eggs, 1/3 cup of the Parmesan cheese, cream, ricotta, cayenne, remaining 1 tbs. oil, salt and pepper. Stir this mixture into the cooked vegetables.

Pour mixture into prepared casserole dish and cover with foil. Pour about 3 inches of boiling water into a roasting pan and set casserole dish in pan. Bake for 30 to 35 minutes, uncover and continue baking for 15 minutes, or until eggs are set. Sprinkle remaining 1/3 cup Parmesan cheese on top and place under broiler until lightly browned.

POULTRY SOUFFLÉ ROLL

Servings: 6–8

This recipe can be made ahead of time and refrigerated or frozen. Simply bring the roll to room temperature, cover with foil and bake in a 375-degree oven for approximately 20 minutes to heat through.

Soufflé:

1/4 cup (1/2 stick) butter
1/2 cup flour
2 cups hot milk
1/2 cup shredded Parmesan cheese
1/2 cup shredded cheddar cheese
1/2 tsp. salt
4 eggs, beaten
4 egg whites
4 slices cheddar cheese

Filling:

2 tbs. butter
1/2 cup chopped onions
1/4 lb. chopped mushrooms
2 pkg. (10 oz. each) frozen chopped spinach, thawed and squeezed dry
1 cup diced cooked chicken or turkey
1 pkg. (3 oz.) cream cheese, softened
1/3 cup sour cream
2 tsp. Dijon mustard
salt and pepper to taste
1 pinch nutmeg

Heat oven to 325°. Line a 10 x15-inch jelly roll pan with parchment (leaving extra paper on the ends). Grease and flour the parchment.

In a heavy saucepan over medium heat, melt butter, stir in flour, and cook 2 minutes, stirring constantly with a whisk. Add milk, blend until smooth and cook until thick. Stir in cheese and salt (sauce will be very stiff), remove pan from the heat. Add a small amount of sauce to beaten eggs and mix well. Add egg mixture to the remaining sauce and stir to combine.

In a large bowl, with a mixer on high speed, beat egg whites until stiff. Fold a dollop of whites into sauce, then fold remaining sauce into egg whites. Pour batter onto prepared pan and spread evenly. Bake 40 to 50 minutes until soufflé is golden brown and springs back when touched.

While soufflé is baking, make filling by melting butter in a skillet and sautéing onion and mushrooms until soft. Stir in spinach, chicken, cream cheese and sour cream until cheese is melted. Add mustard, salt, pepper and nutmeg. Taste and adjust seasonings.

Place a piece of parchment or waxed paper on top of the cooked soufflé and flip soufflé. Peel off bottom sheet of parchment and spread filling over soufflé. Starting with a long side, roll up jelly roll style and place on a greased cookie sheet, seam side down. Cut cheese slices into triangles and lay across the roll to decorate. Place roll under a broiler until cheese melts and is slightly browned. Serve immediately.

EGGPLANT SOUFFLÉ

You will need a 5-cup straight-sided soufflé dish for this recipe. Serve this dish as a breakfast, brunch, lunch or dinner entrée.

¼ cup (½ stick) butter, divided
2 tbs. browned breadcrumbs, divided
1½ lbs. eggplants
2 tbs. olive oil
2 tbs. flour
1 cup milk
salt and white pepper to taste
1 pinch nutmeg
4 egg yolks
¼ cup plus 2 tbs. shredded Parmesan cheese
6 egg whites

Heat oven to 375°. Butter a 5-cup soufflé dish and sprinkle the sides with 1 tbs. of the bread-crumbs. Refrigerate until ready to use.

Trim stems of eggplants and cut in half lengthwise. Run the point of a knife around the inside of the skin and score the flesh. Sprinkle with salt and set aside for 30 minutes. Rinse eggplants with cold water and dry on a paper towel. In a skillet, heat 2 tbs. of the butter and oil and sauté the eggplants, cut sides down, until brown. Transfer eggplants to a cookie sheet and bake for 10 to 15 minutes or until tender. Cool eggplants slightly, then scoop out the flesh and finely chop. Increase oven temperature to 425°.

In a saucepan, melt remaining 2 tbs. butter over medium heat, stir in flour and cook for 1 minute. Whisk in milk and cook until mixture thickens. Add salt, white pepper and nutmeg to taste. Stir in chopped eggplant. Beat in egg yolks, one by one, and cook over low heat, stirring constantly, until mixture thickens slightly. Remove from heat and stir (do not whisk) in 1/4 cup of the Parmesan. Slightly over-season the mixture to accommodate for the egg whites.

In a large bowl, using a mixer on high speed, stiffly whip the egg whites. Add about 1/4 of the egg whites to the warm eggplant mixture and stir until well blended. Add this mixture to the remaining egg whites and fold together very gently. Pour into the prepared soufflé dish. Sprinkle with remaining 1 tbs. Parmesan and remaining 1 tbs. breadcrumbs and bake in the lower third of the oven for about 18 minutes or until the soufflé is puffed and browned. Serve at once.

SALMON AND BROCCOLI SOUFFLÉ

Soufflés are a great low-carbohydrate meal and once you get over the "fear of failure," you will enjoy the light and flavorful results. Serve with a crunchy vegetable salad.

¼ cup (½ stick) butter
3 tbs. finely minced shallots
3 tbs. flour
1 cup hot milk
6 tbs. shredded Parmesan cheese
black pepper to taste
4 egg yolks
½ cup finely chopped cooked salmon
1½ tsp. tomato paste
½ tsp. dried dill
1 cup minced cooked broccoli
¼ tsp. nutmeg
6 egg whites
¼ tsp. salt
¼ tsp. cream of tartar

Heat oven to 400°. Generously butter a 1 1/2-quart soufflé dish and sprinkle with a little shredded Parmesan cheese.

In a skillet over medium heat, melt butter and sauté shallots until translucent. Stir in flour and cook for 2 minutes. Remove from heat and stir in hot milk. Return to heat and cook, stirring, until mixture is thick. Remove from heat and beat in egg yolks, 1/4 cup of the Parmesan cheese, and pepper. Set aside.

In a bowl, combine salmon with tomato paste and dill. Add half the milk-egg mixture. In a separate bowl, combine broccoli with nutmeg and remaining milk-egg mixture. In a large bowl, using a mixer, beat egg whites until they are foamy. Add salt and cream of tartar and beat until stiff, but not dry. Stir a little of the egg whites into the broccoli and salmon mixtures to lighten. Divide the remaining whites evenly between both mixtures and fold in gently.

Spoon half the broccoli mixture into prepared soufflé dish. Gently spread all the salmon mixture over the broccoli mixture, and top with the remaining broccoli mixture. Sprinkle with the remaining 2 tbs. Parmesan cheese. Place in lower third of the oven. Reduce heat to 375° and bake for 35 minutes, until puffed and golden. Serve immediately.

CRAB SOUFFLÉ WITH GUACAMOLE PURÉE

This soufflé is subtle and goes well with a flavorful guacamole purée. This soufflé can also be served with a cheese sauce.

6 oz. crabmeat
2 tbs. unsalted butter
1 cup heavy cream
3 egg yolks

2 tbs. cornstarch
$\frac{1}{2}$ tsp. salt
$\frac{1}{4}$ tsp. dried tarragon
6 egg whites

Heat oven to 375°. Butter a 1-quart soufflé dish.

Squeeze crabmeat dry, reserving liquid. In a skillet over medium heat, melt butter and sauté crabmeat for 1 minute. Remove crab and set aside. Add cream and reserved crab liquid to skillet and bring to a simmer. Mix yolks, cornstarch, salt and tarragon in a small bowl. Add cream mixture to yolks, whisking vigorously. Return mixture to heat and cook, stirring constantly, until mixture thickens. Remove from heat and stir in crab.

In a large bowl, using a mixer, beat whites to stiff peaks and gently fold into crab mixture $\frac{1}{3}$ at a time. Spoon into prepared soufflé dish and set dish in a larger pan. Pour hot water 1 inch deep into large pan. Bake for 45 minutes. Serve immediately with *Guacamole Puree,* page 87.

GUACAMOLE PURÉE

Besides a sauce to accompany the Crab Soufflé, this recipe can be used as a dip for vegetables and crackers, served on scrambled eggs, or as a spread for sandwiches.

4 green onions (mostly white parts)
1–2 cloves garlic
1 large ripe avocado, roughly chopped
2 tsp. fresh lime juice
1 dash Tabasco sauce (or more to taste)

Chop green onions and garlic cloves in a food processor workbowl or blender container. Add avocado, lime juice and Tabasco and process until smooth. Cover and refrigerate until ready to serve.

STUFFED EGGS WITH MUSHROOMS

When you are tired of fried eggs and bacon, spend a little time preparing a better breakfast that will be remembered fondly.

5 tbs. butter, divided
1 tbs. chopped shallots
$1/2$ lb. chopped mushrooms
$1/2$ tsp. salt
$1/8$ tsp. white pepper
$1/4$ cup flour
$2 1/2$ cups hot milk
1 cup shredded Swiss or Gruyère cheese, divided
10 hard-cooked eggs, peeled
$1/4$ cup finely minced fresh parsley

Heat oven to 425°. Melt 2 tbs. of the butter in a skillet over medium heat and sauté shallots until soft. Add mushrooms and cook until they are dry, 3 to 5 minutes. Season with salt and pepper. In a saucepan over medium heat, melt remaining 3 tbs. butter, add flour and cook for 2 minutes. Take off heat and whisk in milk. Return to heat and simmer until thick. Add 1/2 cup of the cheese and stir until melted and smooth.

Butter a 9 x 13-inch baking pan. Cut eggs lengthwise in half and remove yolks. Push yolks through a sieve. In a large bowl, combine yolks, mushrooms, 1/3 cup of the cheese sauce and parsley. Cut a thin slice from the bottom of egg whites so the eggs will not slide. Spread bottom of baking dish with a small amount of the sauce.

Fill egg whites with yolk-mushroom mixture and arrange in the prepared pan. Top with remaining sauce and sprinkle with remaining 1/2 cup cheese. Bake until bubbly and slightly brown.

EGGS IN ONION SAUCE

Onions are healthy for you and loaded with flavor. This dish can be made the day before and warmed just before serving.

6 large eggs
2 tbs. butter
4 medium onions
1 tsp. dried thyme
$\frac{1}{2}$ tsp. salt
$\frac{1}{8}$ tsp. nutmeg
1 pinch white pepper
1 tbs. minced fresh parsley
3 tbs. flour
2 cups half-and-half
1 cup shredded Gruyère cheese

Over medium heat, place eggs in a saucepan with cold water to cover and bring to a simmer. Simmer for 10 minutes. Remove from the heat and plunge eggs in cold water. When cool, peel eggs and slice into quarters lengthwise. Arrange them in one layer in a 7 x 10-inch pan. Heat oven to 450°.

Cut onions in half and thinly slice. In a skillet, melt butter over medium heat. Add onions to skillet along with thyme, salt, nutmeg and pepper and cook until onions are tender but not brown, about 20 minutes. Sprinkle with parsley and flour and stir to coat. Reduce heat to low and cook for 2 minutes, stirring constantly. Add half-and-half and cook, stirring frequently, until sauce thickens, about 5 minutes. Taste and adjust seasonings. Cover the eggs with onion sauce and sprinkle top with cheese. Bake for about 10 minutes until heated through, then place under a broiler to brown the cheese. Serve hot.

SPINACH FRITTATA

Fresh spinach is always preferred but one 10-ounce package of frozen chopped spinach can be substituted. Make sure you thaw and thoroughly squeeze the spinach dry before using.

1 bunch fresh spinach, washed, stems
  removed
1 bunch green onions, chopped
1/4 cup dry (powdered) milk
1/2 cup water
2 eggs

1/2 tsp. salt
1/4 tsp. dried tarragon
1/3 cup shredded Parmesan cheese, divided
1 large tomato, thinly sliced
sour cream or plain yogurt, for garnish

Heat oven to 350°. Butter a 9-inch pie pan. Place spinach in a large skillet along with onions and cook over medium-high heat, stirring, for 1 minute until spinach is barely wilted. Transfer spinach and onions to a blender container along with dry milk, water, eggs, salt, tarragon and half the Parmesan cheese. Blend until finely minced. Pour into prepared pie pan and arrange tomato slices on top. Sprinkle with the remaining cheese and bake for 30 minutes or until set. Cut into wedges and serve with a dollop of sour cream or plain yogurt.

SHRIMP OMELET

This simple omelet is flavorful and easy to prepare. Crabmeat can be substituted for the shrimp. Also, fresh cilantro can be substituted for the parsley.

2 tbs. olive oil
3 tbs. butter, divided
½ lb. shrimp, peeled and deveined
2 cloves garlic, minced
2 tbs. minced fresh parsley
1 tbs. fresh lemon juice

4 eggs, beaten
¼ tsp. salt
1 pinch pepper
shredded Parmesan or Gruyère cheese,
   optional

In a skillet, heat oil and 2 tbs. of the butter over medium-high heat. Sauté shrimp until just tender and pink, add garlic and cook 1 minute longer. Stir in parsley and lemon juice and set aside.

In a large bowl, beat together eggs, salt and pepper. Melt remaining 1 tbs. butter in a separate skillet and gently cook eggs over low heat without stirring until firm but still moist. Spoon shrimp mixture over top and fold omelet over filling in a cigar shape. Sprinkle with cheese, if desired. Serve hot.

MUSHROOM SOUFFLÉ

Worcestershire sauce greatly enhances the flavor of mushrooms. Consider using a mixture of different mushrooms for fun.

2 tbs. butter
1 small onion, finely minced
1/4 lb. fresh mushrooms, sliced
4 large eggs, separated
1 can (10 oz.) condensed cream of mushroom
   soup

2 tbs. quick-cooking tapioca
1 tsp. dry mustard
1 tsp. Worcestershire sauce
1/2 tsp. cream of tartar

Heat oven to 400°. Lightly grease a soufflé dish. In a skillet over medium-high heat, melt butter and sauté onion and mushrooms until soft. In a saucepan, combine mushroom mixture, egg yolks, cream of mushroom soup, tapioca, mustard and Worcestershire sauce. Set aside for 5 minutes. Heat mixture over low heat and simmer for 5 minutes, stirring constantly. Cool mixture to room temperature. In a large bowl, using a mixer, beat egg whites with cream of tartar until stiff. Fold whites into mushroom mixture. Pour into prepared soufflé dish. Set soufflé dish in a larger pan. Pour hot water 2 inches deep into larger pan. Bake for 45 minutes and serve immediately.

HARVEST FRITTATA

A frittata is similar to an omelet but the fillings are mixed into the eggs and baked. If the baked eggs need a little more color, simply broil for 1 minute to brown the cheese just before serving.

½ pkg. sesame crisp wafers
1 cup milk
2 tbs. olive oil
1 large onion, chopped
½ lb. mushrooms, sliced
2–3 cloves garlic, minced

2 bunches fresh spinach, cleaned and dried
2 stalks broccoli, steamed and chopped
⅓ lb. feta cheese, crumbled
1 pint cottage cheese
1 cup shredded Parmesan cheese
12 eggs, beaten

Heat oven to 375°. Oil a 9 x 13-inch baking pan. Crush crackers into a bowl and add milk. Heat oil over medium heat in a skillet and sauté onions, mushrooms, and garlic until vegetables are soft. In a large bowl, combine the sautéed vegetables with spinach and broccoli. Add soaked crackers, feta, cottage cheese and Parmesan. Stir in beaten eggs., pour egg mixture into prepared pan and bake for 35 minutes until frittata is set and browned.

CHEESE ROLL WITH MUSHROOMS

This cheese soufflé is baked flat, filled with a mushroom mixture and rolled jelly roll style. Any sautéed vegetable could be substituted for the mushrooms.

¼ cup (½ stick) butter, divided
2 tbs. flour
1 cup milk
5 eggs, separated
1 cup shredded Parmesan cheese
1 tbs. chopped shallots
½ lb. mushrooms, chopped
salt and pepper to taste

Heat oven to 350°. Oil a 10 x 15-inch jelly roll pan, line with waxed or parchment paper and oil the paper. Melt 2 tbs. of the butter in a saucepan over medium-high heat and stir in flour. Cook for 2 minutes, add milk and cook, stirring, until mixture thickens. Set aside to cool for 5 minutes.

In a small bowl, beat egg yolks and add to milk mixture. In a large bowl, using a mixer, beat eggs whites until stiff. Fold 1/3 of the egg whites into sauce to lighten, and then gently fold in the remaining whites. Fold in Parmesan cheese and spread in prepared jelly roll pan. Bake for 15 minutes.

While the soufflé is baking, melt remaining 2 tbs. butter in a skillet and sauté shallots until soft. Add mushrooms and cook until they are dry, about 10 minutes. Season with salt and pepper.

Remove soufflé from oven and turn out onto parchment or waxed paper. Remove oiled paper from soufflé, Spread soufflé with mushroom mixture. Starting with one long side, roll up jelly roll-style and serve either hot or at room temperature.

OMELET PIPÉRADE

Pipérade means a Basque dish, always made with tomatoes and peppers in olive oil. These wonderful individual omelets are loaded with a colorful mixture of tomatoes and bell peppers. This would be great served with a thick slab of country ham or pepper bacon.

3 tbs. oil
1 medium onion, thinly sliced
1 tomato, peeled, seeded and chopped
2 cloves garlic, minced
1 green bell pepper, diced

salt and pepper to taste
8 eggs
¼ cup (½ stick) butter
¼–½ cup shredded Parmesan cheese, for
   garnish, optional

Heat oil over medium heat in a skillet and cook onions until soft but not brown. Add tomato, garlic, salt and pepper and cook until mixture is thick and pulpy. Add bell pepper and cook 5 minutes more. Taste and adjust seasonings. In a small bowl, beat 2 of the eggs. Melt 1 tbs. of the butter in a small skillet and cook eggs gently over low heat until just barely set. Place about 2 tbs. of filling in the center of each omelet and fold over. Repeat with remaining eggs, butter and filling to create 3 more omelets. Serve at once. If desired, sprinkle 1 to 2 tbs. shredded Parmesan cheese over each omelet before serving.

MAIN DISHES

SPICY GINGER BEEF

For a different flavor, substitute 1 tablespoon finely chopped lemongrass in place of the ginger. Be careful in handling jalapeños—wear gloves and never rub your eyes. The amount of jalapeño is totally optional.

3–4 tbs. safflower oil
3 large cloves garlic
1/2–1 jalapeño pepper, thinly sliced and
　seeded
1-inch piece fresh ginger, peeled and cut into
　small julienne strips
1 lb. beef tenderloin or top sirloin

1 tbs. cornstarch
1 tbs. oyster sauce
1 tbs. lime juice
2 tbs. chopped green onions, for garnish
2–3 tbs. chopped fresh cilantro, for garnish
1/4 cup diced red bell pepper, for garnish

Heat oil in a large skillet or wok over medium-high heat and add garlic, jalapeño pepper and ginger and stir-fry until vegetables are softened. Remove vegetables and set aside. Cut beef into thin strips, dust with cornstarch and stir-fry for 2 minutes. Return the vegetables to skillet with beef, add oyster sauce and lime juice, cook for 1 minute longer until sauce is slightly thickened. Garnish with green onions, cilantro and red bell pepper.

HAZELNUT CHICKEN

Hazelnuts and sesame seeds give a delicious toasty and crunchy texture to chicken and can be served with most bottled low carbohydrate sauces. I would recommend serving this with Chutney Cream Sauce, page 118.

6 chicken breast halves, skinned and bones
salt and pepper to taste
1 cup flour
3 eggs, beaten
$1/3$ cup cold water

$1^1/2$ cups finely chopped toasted hazelnuts
1 cup sesame seeds
3 tbs. olive or hazelnut oil
2 tbs. butter

Place each chicken breast between 2 pieces of waxed paper and pound until meat is about $1/2$-inch thick. Liberally sprinkle salt and pepper on both sides of chicken and dredge in flour. In a shallow bowl, beat eggs with cold water. In a second shallow bowl, combine hazelnuts with sesame seeds. Dip dredged chicken in egg mixture, then in hazelnut mixture. Heat olive oil and butter in a large skillet over medium heat. Sauté chicken, in batches if necessary, until browned on both sides and cooked through, about 3 minutes per side. Serve immediately.

SESAME SEED FISH

Sesame seeds add wonderful flavor and crunch to ordinary fish. Use untoasted sesame seeds on the fish, because sautéing will toast the sesame seeds naturally.

1 lb. white fish fillets (halibut, bass, red
   snapper)
1/4 cup dry sherry or white wine
1 tbs. minced fresh ginger
3 green onions, finely minced
1/2 tsp. salt

1/2 cup cornstarch
1 egg, beaten
2 tbs. cold water
1 cup sesame seeds
3 tbs. vegetable oil
1 tbs. sesame oil

Cut fish into bite-sized pieces. In a shallow bowl, combine sherry, ginger, green onions and salt. Place fish in sherry mixture and marinate for 30 minutes to 1 hour in the refrigerator. Remove fish from marinade and dredge in cornstarch. Mix egg with water in a shallow bowl. Pour sesame seeds into another shallow bowl. Dip dredged fish in egg mixture and then in sesame seeds. Heat vegetable oil and sesame oil in a large skillet over medium heat. Add fish, in batches if necessary, and gently sauté until fish is golden and flaky.

CHICKEN AND PINE NUTS

I generally serve this dish over pasta or rice. This recipe was modified to use steamed cauliflower in place of the pasta. One pound of shelled and deveined prawns can be substituted for the chicken.

1 small head cauliflower
1 lb. fresh asparagus
1/3 cup sesame seeds
1 cup pine nuts
3 tbs. vegetable oil
2 tbs. sesame oil

2 tbs. minced fresh ginger
4 cloves garlic, minced
1 lb. skinless, boneless chicken breasts, cubed
1/3 cup dry sherry
4 green onions, chopped
salt and pepper to taste

Finely chop the cauliflower and steam or boil until tender, about 6 minutes. Set aside. Break off and discard tough ends of asparagus. Steam asparagus until just barely cooked. Cut into 1-inch pieces. In a dry skillet over medium heat, toast sesame seeds and pine nuts, stirring constantly. Remove from skillet and set aside. Heat vegetable oil and sesame oil in a wok or skillet over medium-high heat. Add ginger, garlic and chicken and stir-fry for 2 minutes. Add sherry and asparagus and cook for 1 minute. Add cauliflower, sesame seeds, pine nuts and green onions and stir-fry until heated through. Add salt and pepper and serve immediately.

SCALLOP AND PRAWN SENSATION

Servings: 4

This tomato-based concoction is best served over couscous, pasta or rice. To reduce the carbohydrate count, I like to serve it over steamed chopped cauliflower or steamed spaghetti squash.

2 large leeks
2 tbs. olive oil
4 cloves garlic, minced
$1/2$ tsp. crushed red pepper flakes
1 large carrot, diced
$3/4$ tsp. ground cumin
$1/4$ tsp. cinnamon
$1/8$ tsp. cayenne pepper

$1^1/_2$ tsp. salt
$1^1/_2$ cup chopped tomatoes (fresh or canned), including liquid
1 cup dry white wine
1 cup water
$3/4$ lb. medium prawns, peeled and deveined
$3/4$ lb. medium scallops
$1/4$ cup chopped fresh cilantro

Trim the tough dark green tops of the leeks and discard. Split the leeks in half lengthwise, rinse well to remove sand and cut into $1/2$-inch dice. Heat oil in a heavy saucepan over medium heat. Add leeks and garlic and sauté until leeks are tender. Add red pepper flakes, carrots, cumin, cinnamon, cayenne and salt, reduce heat to medium-low and sauté until carrots are tender. Add tomatoes, wine and water, increase heat to medium, bring to a boil and cook 5 minutes. Stir in prawns and scallops and cook until they just become opaque; do not overcook. Remove from heat and stir in cilantro. Serve immediately.

SPINACH AND CHICKEN SATAY

Swiss chard or beet greens can be used in place of the spinach. Tofu can be substituted for the chicken. Use only fresh spinach in this recipe.

1 cup *Satay Peanut Sauce,* page 119
1 large whole chicken breast, cooked
2 lbs. fresh spinach, cleaned and stems removed
crushed red pepper flakes to taste
2 tbs. finely chopped roasted peanuts
1/4 cup chopped fresh cilantro

In a small saucepan over low heat, warm *Satay Peanut Sauce.*

Cut chicken into large dice. Place a large pot of water over high heat and bring to boiling. Immerse the spinach into the boiling water for 15 seconds, remove, drain and place on serving platter. Cover with cooked chicken and pour hot Satay Sauce on top. Sprinkle with red pepper flakes, peanuts and cilantro.

SALMON WITH HORSERADISH CREAM

If you are unable to find crème fraiche, you can use heavy cream mixed with a little sour cream instead. The salmon fillets should be about 1 inch thick and very fresh.

¾ cup crème fraiche
1 tbs. prepared horseradish sauce
1¼ tsp. fresh lemon juice (or to taste)
salt and pepper to taste
3 tbs. butter

3 tart green apples
½ tsp. cinnamon
2 tbs. peanut oil
6 salmon fillets with skin, 6 oz. each

Heat oven to 425°. In a bowl, whip crème fraiche until soft peaks form. Fold in horseradish, lemon juice, salt and pepper. Taste and adjust seasonings. Set aside.

Melt butter in a skillet over medium-high heat. Peel, core and cut apples into (julienne) match-stick pieces. Add apples and cinnamon to skillet and cook until just tender, about 5 minutes.

Heat oil in another heavy skillet over high heat. Add salmon, skin side down, and cook until the skin is crisp and golden, about 3 minutes.

Season salmon with salt and pepper. Oil a cookie sheet, place salmon (skin side up) on cookie sheet and bake about 5 minutes, until salmon is opaque in the center. Divide apple mixture among the serving plates, cover with a salmon fillet and top with horseradish cream.

EGGPLANT CASSEROLE

The skin of eggplants is edible and adds great color to the dish. However, some people don't like the texture, so remove the skin if you prefer.

1 medium eggplant, sliced lengthwise into ½-inch thick slices

⅓ cup olive oil, divided

salt and pepper to taste

1 medium onion, chopped

3 cloves garlic, minced

3 medium tomatoes, peeled, seeded and chopped

1 tsp. sugar

1 tsp. dried basil

½ cup ricotta cheese

1 egg

⅓ cup plus 2 tbs. shredded Parmesan cheese, divided

½ cup heavy cream

1 pinch ground allspice

1 pinch nutmeg

1 tbs. chopped fresh parsley

Heat broiler. Brush eggplant with half the oil, then sprinkle with salt and pepper. Place on a cookie sheet and broil until slices are softened and lightly browned. Set aside.

In a skillet over medium-high heat, add remaining oil and cook onion and garlic until soft. Add tomatoes, sugar, salt, pepper and basil. Reduce heat and simmer uncovered for about 20 minutes or until sauce has thickened.

Heat oven to 450°. Arrange half the eggplant slices in a well-buttered shallow baking dish. Spread tomato sauce over eggplant and top with remaining eggplant. In a bowl, stir ricotta cheese, egg and ⅓ cup of the Parmesan cheese together. Gradually stir in cream until mixture is a thick pouring consistency. Season with salt, allspice, nutmeg, and parsley. Pour over eggplant and sprinkle with remaining 2 tbs. Parmesan cheese. Bake for 10 minutes, reduce heat to 375° and bake for 20 minutes longer or until golden brown and firm to the touch.

VEGETARIAN MANICOTTI

Manicotti is large shell-shaped pasta that can be stuffed with a variety of fillings. This vegetarian version is tasty and healthy. If you wish to add more protein to your meal, serve the manicotti with Favorite Ragu Sauce, *page 116*

¼ cup olive oil, divided
1 small onion, minced
1 can (15 oz.) plum tomatoes, including liquid
1 can (6 oz.) tomato paste
1 tsp. sugar
1½ tsp. dried basil, divided
1 tsp. salt, divided
¼ cup water
3 cloves garlic, minced

1 lb. eggplant, peeled and diced
1 medium zucchini, diced
¼ lb. mushrooms, diced
1 pkg. (8 oz.) manicotti shells
1½ cups shredded mozzarella cheese, divided
1 cup ricotta cheese
1 egg, beaten

In a large saucepan over medium heat add 2 tbs. of the oil and sauté onions until soft. Coarsely chop tomatoes and stir into onion with tomato paste, sugar, 1 tsp. of the basil, ½ tsp. of the salt and water. Bring mixture to a boil, then reduce heat to low, cover and simmer for 30 minutes.

In a skillet over medium-high heat, add remaining 2 tbs. oil and sauté garlic, eggplant, zucchini and mushrooms for 5 minutes. Cover and cook for 10 minutes or until vegetables are tender. Remove from heat and cool to room temperature.

Cook manicotti shells according to package directions. Heat oven to 375°. In a bowl, combine 1 cup of the mozzarella cheese, ricotta cheese, egg, remaining 1/2 tsp. basil, and remaining 1/2 tsp. salt. Combine with sautéed vegetable mixture. Fill cooked manicotti shells with cheese-vegetable mixture. Spread a thin layer of tomato sauce on bottom of a 9 x13-inch baking dish. Arrange stuffed shells over sauce, pour remaining sauce over the shells and sprinkle with remaining 1/2 cup mozzarella cheese. Cover dish loosely with foil and bake 45 minutes or until hot.

CRAB MORNAY

Mornay sauce is a creamy cheese sauce that can be used in a variety of dishes. Shrimp, scallops and even white fish can be substituted for the crab.

5 tbs. butter
1/4 cup finely chopped green onions
1 cup sliced fresh mushrooms
1/4 cup flour
1 cup heavy cream
1/4 cup dry white wine
1/4 cup dry sherry
1 cup Jack cheese, shredded
1/2 tsp. salt

1 pinch nutmeg
1/4 tsp. pepper
1 tsp. lemon juice
3/4 lb. snow crabmeat
6–8 canned artichoke hearts, drained
1 cup soft breadcrumbs
2 tbs. melted butter
paprika, for garnish

Heat oven to 350°. In a skillet over medium heat, melt butter and sauté green onions and mushrooms until soft. Stir in flour and cook for 1 minute. Slowly blend in cream, white wine and sherry. Simmer for 2 minutes until sauce thickens. Add cheese, salt, nutmeg, pepper and lemon juice, stirring until cheese is melted and sauce is smooth. Stir in crabmeat and artichoke hearts until thoroughly combined.

Transfer crab mixture to a casserole dish. Toss breadcrumbs with melted butter. Sprinkle over top of crab-artichoke mixture and sprinkle with paprika. Bake for 20 to 25 minutes or until breadcrumbs are golden brown. Serve immediately.

MAPLE PORK MEDALLIONS

Boneless pork loins are one of the great secrets to fast cooking. Simply cut loin into round medallions and sauté quickly over high heat. For richness of flavor, use only pure maple syrup.

1¼ lb. boneless pork loin
pepper to taste
2 tbs. butter
1 tsp. olive oil
¼ cup minced shallots or onions

2 tsp. Dijon mustard
1 cup chicken broth
2 tbs. pure maple syrup
2 tbs. balsamic vinegar

Cut pork loin into medallions (slices) 8 ½-inch thick. Place medallions between waxed paper and flatten slightly with a meat mallet. Sprinkle both sides of medallions with pepper. Heat butter and olive oil in a large skillet over medium-high heat. Sauté pork until brown and cooked through, about 3 to 4 minutes per side. Transfer pork to a plate and add shallots to skillet. Cook until shallots soften. Add mustard and chicken broth and simmer for about 5 minutes. Stir in maple syrup and vinegar and simmer 5 minutes longer. Taste sauce and adjust seasonings. Return pork (and any juice from pork) to skillet and cook for about 1 minute or until just heated through. Serve immediately.

SAUCES

FAVORITE RAGU SAUCE

This sauce is loaded with meat. Use any combination of meats for variety. If desired, serve the meat separately and use the sauce over pasta or steamed vegetables.

3 tbs. olive oil
1 large onion, chopped
6 cloves garlic, minced
1½ lb. ground chuck
¾ lb. ground pork
1 lb. beef bones
1 lb. pork chops
1 lb. beef or pork ribs
½ cup red wine
2 cans (28 oz. each) tomatoes, including liquid
2 small cans tomato paste
1 tbs. dried oregano
1 tsp. sugar, or more to taste
1 tsp. dried basil
salt and pepper to taste

In a heavy stockpot, heat olive oil over medium-high heat and sauté onions until they are soft. Add ground chuck and pork and cook, stirring, until meat is browned. Remove meat mixture from pot and set aside.

Add bones, chops and ribs and brown on all sides. Add wine and deglaze pan by stirring vigorously to remove browned bits on bottom of pan. Return ground meat mixture to pan along with tomatoes, tomato paste, oregano, sugar, basil, salt and pepper. Bring mixture to a low boil, reduce heat and simmer for 3 to 4 hours, stirring frequently.

Remove bones, ribs and chops from sauce. Shred meat from ribs and pork chops. Discard bones and return meat to sauce. Adjust seasonings to taste.

CHUTNEY CREAM SAUCE

Makes 3 cups

This is one of my favorite sauces, which goes well with all types of poultry. It can also be served over steamed vegetables, rice or pasta.

¼ cup (½ stick) butter
½ cup chopped onion
1–2 large Golden Delicious apples, peeled and chopped
¾ cup mango chutney
1 cup heavy cream
1 tsp. Dijon mustard
½ tsp. curry powder
salt and pepper to taste

Heat butter in skillet, add onion and sauté until they are soft. Add apples and sauté until the are soft. Stir in chutney and cream and cook until mixture begins to thicken. Add mustard, curry powder, salt and pepper, taste and adjust seasonings. Serve hot.

SATAY PEANUT SAUCE

This is a great sauce for vegetables and poultry. It can also be used with beef and pork satay. I like to serve this sauce over fresh steamed spinach or other greens.

2 tbs. vegetable oil
3 cloves garlic, crushed
1 cup water
1–2 red jalapeño peppers, finely chopped
¼ cup lime juice
1 tsp. salt
2 tbs. honey, Splenda, or brown sugar
2 tbs. soy sauce
1 cup smooth unsweetened peanut butter
1 can (14 oz.) coconut milk

In a small saucepan, heat oil over medium heat, add garlic and sauté until it softens, about 30 seconds. Add water, jalapeños, lime juice, salt, honey, soy sauce, peanut butter and coconut milk and stir well. Reduce heat and simmer for about 10 minutes, stirring frequently with a whisk, until thick.

GREEN YOGURT SAUCE

This low-fat sauce is great to serve on seafood, vegetables, and potatoes and can be used as a dip. The beautiful green color comes from watercress.

1 bunch watercress, trimmed
3/4 cup plain low-fat yogurt
2 tbs. sour cream (low-fat if desired)
1 tsp. fresh lemon juice
1 tsp. white wine vinegar
1 tsp. Dijon mustard
salt and pepper to taste

In a saucepan lined with a steamer basket, steam watercress until just barely wilted. Remove and immediately plunge in ice water to bring back the bright green color. Squeeze watercress dry. Puree watercress in a food processor workbowl. Add yogurt, sour cream, lemon juice, vinegar, mustard, salt and pepper and process until smooth. Taste and adjust seasonings. Refrigerate until ready to use.

CUCUMBER SAUCE

This is a great sauce to serve alongside a salmon mousse, with most fish dishes and as a refreshing dip for vegetables.

1 cucumber, peeled, grated
1 cup sour cream
1 tsp. fresh dill weed
1 tsp. capers, drained
1 tsp. Dijon mustard
1 tbs. fresh lemon juice
1 tsp. grated onion
$\frac{1}{2}$ tsp. salt (or to taste)

Place cucumber in a colander and drain for at least 30 minutes. Squeeze grated cucumber to remove excess liquid. Place cucumber, sour cream, dill, capers, mustard, lemon juice, onion and salt in a food processor workbowl or blender container and pulse to combine. Refrigerate until ready to serve.

SHRIMP SAUCE

This sauce is best served over seafood like shrimp, lobster, or scallops. I've used it as a shrimp cocktail sauce and served it alongside fried fish.

1 large clove garlic
1 cup mayonnaise
1/2 cup bottled mild chili sauce
1 tbs. horseradish sauce, or to taste
2 tsp. fresh lime juice
1/2 tsp. dry mustard
1/8 tsp. cayenne pepper

Mash garlic with a knife or press through a garlic press and add to a bowl with mayonnaise, chili sauce, horseradish, lime juice, mustard and cayenne. Stir well and adjust seasonings. Cover and refrigerate for at least 4 hours before serving.

ONION AND GORGONZOLA SAUCE

Use this great sauce with pasta or over cooked spaghetti squash. It can also be served over cooked poultry, beef or pork.

1/4 cup olive oil
2 large sweet onions, chopped
3 cloves garlic, minced
2 tbs. balsamic vinegar
1/2 tsp. salt
1/4 tsp. pepper
4–6 oz. Gorgonzola cheese, crumbled

Heat oil in a skillet over medium-high heat. Add onions and sauté until onions are soft and slightly browned, about 5 minutes. Add garlic and cook 1 minute. Remove skillet from heat and stir in vinegar, salt and pepper. If serving on pasta, stir onion mixture with pasta, sprinkle cheese on top and toss. If serving over meat, pile onion mixture on cooked meat and sprinkle cheese on top.

BEARNAISE SAUCE

A French classic, bearnaise sauce is great served on all kinds of steamed vegetables as well as poached eggs and meats like ham or poultry.

1/2 cup tarragon wine vinegar
1 bay leaf
6 peppercorns
1 pinch ground mace
1 pinch dried thyme
4 large egg yolks
1 tsp. arrowroot or cornstarch
1 cup (2 sticks) butter, melted
2 tbs. minced fresh parsley
1 1/2 tbs. chopped shallots
2 tsp. dried tarragon
1/2 tsp. minced garlic
1/4 tsp. tomato paste
1 pinch cayenne pepper
few drops of Kitchen Bouquet, optional

Place vinegar with bay leaf, peppercorns, mace and thyme in a small saucepan over medium-high heat. Cook until vinegar is reduced by half. Strain into a small bowl, discarding solids, and set aside. Place egg yolks and arrow-root in food processor workbowl or blender container and process until yolks turn a pale yellow. Melt butter in a small saucepan. Slowly pour hot melted butter onto egg yolks while the machine is running. When sauce thickens to the consistency of heavy cream, add reserved vinegar mixture along with parsley, shallots, tarragon, garlic, tomato paste, cayenne and Kitchen Bouquet, if using. Taste and adjust seasonings. Serve immediately.

MUSHROOM CREAM SAUCE

Serve this delicious sauce over toasted bread rounds for a starter course, or over poached eggs for a unique breakfast treat. This sauce also goes well with beef.

1 cup (2 sticks) butter
1/2 lb. fresh mushrooms, sliced
1/2 cup dry white wine
1 cup beef broth

1 cup heavy cream
1/4 cup chopped fresh chives
salt and pepper to taste

Melt butter in a saucepan over medium-high heat. Pour into a clear glass measuring cup. Butter will separate into 3 layers. Skim off top foamy layer and discard. Slowly pour the clear center layer into a separate container and discard solids on the bottom. The center layer is clarified butter.

Heat 1/2 cup of the clarified butter in a skillet over medium-high heat. Add mushrooms and sauté until mushrooms absorb the butter, stirring frequently. Pour in wine and bring mixture to a boil. Add beef broth and stir to combine. Reduce heat to medium, add cream and stir until blended. Stir in chives, salt and pepper and continue to cook until sauce is creamy and thickened.

ALMOND ORANGE SAUCE

This unusual sauce is great served on rice dishes, over spaghetti squash, served with cooked poultry or as a dip for vegetables or chicken nuggets. Almond butter is available at specialty stores or health food stores.

1 cup almond butter
½ cup boiling water
½ cup orange juice
1 tbs. soy sauce
1 tsp. minced fresh ginger
1 tsp. grated orange rind
salt to taste

In a bowl, mix almond butter with boiling water until smooth. Add orange juice, soy sauce, ginger, orange rind and salt. Taste and adjust seasonings. Serve hot or at room temperature.

YOGURT DILL SAUCE

Makes 3½ cups

This is a great sauce to serve with seafood or as a dressing for seafood pasta salad. It also can be used as a dip for vegetables or crackers.

3 cups plain yogurt
5 tbs. minced fresh dill (or 5 tsp. dried)
5 tbs. minced green onions
1 tbs. minced garlic
3 tbs. fresh lemon juice
few drops Tabasco sauce
lemon slices, for garnish
chopped fresh parsley, for garnish

In a bowl, combine yogurt, dill, green onions, garlic, lemon juice and Tabasco. Taste and adjust seasonings. Refrigerate until ready to serve. Garnish with lemon slices and parsley just before serving.

128   SAUCES

ROQUEFORT SAUCE

This simple sauce goes very well with beef or poultry. This recipe can also be used as a dip or salad dressing.

1 cup mayonnaise
1 cup sour cream
1 tsp. garlic salt
1 tsp. celery salt
2 tbs. lemon juice
4 oz. Roquefort cheese, crumbled

Place mayonnaise, sour cream, garlic salt, celery salt, lemon juice in a bowl and mix well. Add Roquefort and stir to combine. Do not use a blender or mixer; the sauce should not be smooth. Taste and adjust seasonings. Refrigerate until ready to serve.

CREAMY PEA SAUCE

This simple sauce is perfect served over pasta or poultry dishes. Consider using this sauce as a base for chicken pot pie or simply over cooked vegetables and diced cooked chicken. If you plan to serve it with pasta, melt a few tablespoons of butter and toss with pasta before adding the sauce.

1 1/2 cups heavy cream
nutmeg to taste
6 slices prosciutto, chopped
3/4 cup fresh peas, or frozen peas, thawed
1/2 cup shredded Parmesan cheese

In a saucepan, heat cream over medium-high heat until it thickens. Add nutmeg, prosciutto, peas, and 1/4 cup of the Parmesan cheese. Stir until combined. Pour sauce over meat, vegetables or pasta and sprinkle with remaining 1/4 cup Parmesan cheese.

LEMON SAUCE

Use this simple, sweet sauce as an accompaniment to a dessert soufflé or over fresh fruit.

1½ cups cold water, divided
½ cup sugar or Splenda
4 tsp. cornstarch
2 tsp. pure vanilla extract
¼ cup fresh lemon juice

In a heavy saucepan over medium-high heat, boil 1 cup of the water and sugar, stirring, until sugar is dissolved. In a small bowl, mix cornstarch with remaining ½ cup cold water and stir into sugar mixture. Cook, stirring constantly, until mixture thickens, remove from heat and stir in vanilla and lemon juice. Serve warm or refrigerate and serve cold.

FRUIT SAUCE

This quick sauce recipe can work with all types of berries. The amount of sugar varies considerably depending on the brand used. Use fresh berries whenever possible. Frozen berries require more sugar.

1 pint fresh raspberries or strawberries, or 1 pkg. (10 oz.) frozen raspberries or strawberries, thawed
2 tbs. sugar
¹/₂ cup Splenda sugar (or to taste)

Place berries in a food processor work-bowl or blender container. Add sugar, process until smooth, then taste and determine how much Splenda you wish to add for desired sweetness. Force mixture through a sieve to remove seeds. Refrigerate until ready to use.

DESSERTS

SIMPLE DESSERT SOUFFLÉ

This high-protein dessert has a subtle lemon flavor that goes well with Fruit Sauce, *page 132. This recipe should be baked in a shallow glass or ceramic baking dish.*

6 large eggs, separated
1 tbs. flour
2 tsp. freshly grated lemon zest
$\frac{1}{2}$ tsp. cream of tartar
2 tbs. sugar
2 tbs. Splenda sugar

Heat oven to 425°. Butter a $1\frac{1}{2}$–2-quart shallow baking dish and sprinkle with sugar.

In a medium bowl, using a mixer, beat egg yolks, and then beat in flour and lemon zest. In a large bowl, using a mixer, beat egg whites until they are foamy and add cream of tartar. Continue beating and gradually add the sugar and Splenda until egg whites are stiff and shiny. Pour yolk mixture over whites and fold in lightly. Pour into prepared baking dish and bake for 10 to 12 minutes until puffed and brown. Serve immediately with a fruit sauce.

SOUFFLÉ GRAND MARNIER

This is a delicious, high-protein dessert that has a subtle orange flavor. For variety, try using other fruit-flavored liqueurs in place of the Grand Marnier.

1 cup whole milk
¼ cup sugar or Splenda, divided
¼ cup flour
3 egg yolks

grated zest of 2 oranges
¼ cup Grand Marnier liqueur
5 egg whites

Heat oven to 425°. Butter a 4-cup soufflé mold and sprinkle with a little sugar. In a small saucepan, bring milk almost to a boil; set aside. In a bowl, blend 2 tbs. sugar and flour together. Beat in egg yolks and orange zest. Whisk in hot milk. Return mixture to saucepan and bring to a boil, stirring constantly. Cook until mixture thickens. Remove from heat, cool slightly, then stir in liqueur.

In a large bowl, using a mixer, beat egg whites until they begin to hold shape, sprinkle with 1 tbs. of the sugar and continue beating until stiff. Add remaining 1 tbs. sugar and beat until glossy. Beat milk mixture with ¼ of the beaten whites. Pour over remaining whites and gently fold together. Spoon mixture into prepared soufflé dish (not more than ¾ full) and bake 12 to 15 minutes. Serve immediately.

STRAWBERRY COEUR A LA CRÈME

This creamy dessert is high in protein and low in sugar. Other berries, such as raspberries, blueberries or blackberries, can be substituted for the strawberries. The amount of sugar will vary according to the sweetness of the berries used.

1 pint strawberries, hulled
2 tbs. dry red wine
$\frac{1}{3}$ cup plus 3 tbs. sugar or Splenda, divided
8 oz. cream cheese, softened
1 cup whole-milk cottage cheese
$\frac{1}{4}$ cup heavy cream
$1\frac{1}{4}$ tsp. vanilla extract
fresh mint sprigs, for garnish

Dice strawberries and reserve ⅓ cup for garnish. Place the remaining strawberries in a saucepan along with wine and 3 tbs. of the sugar. Bring the mixture to a boil, then reduce heat to a simmer and cook for 20 minutes, stirring occasionally. Force the sauce through a sieve and refrigerate until ready to use.

Line six ½-cup heart-shaped molds or custard cups with 6-inch squares of moistened triple-thick cheesecloth, allowing the cloth to hang over the edge. In a food processor workbowl or blender container, process cream cheese, cottage cheese, cream, vanilla and remaining ⅓ cup sugar until smooth. Fill the molds with the cheese mixture, folding the excess cheesecloth over the top. Set molds in a jelly roll pan to catch excess liquid. Refrigerate overnight. Spread strawberry sauce on 6 serving plates and top each with an unmolded coeur a la crème. Sprinkle diced strawberries around plate and garnish with mint sprigs.

SPICED MELON BALLS

This light, refreshing finish to a meal is easy to prepare and can be enriched with a dollop of sweetened whipped cream on top. This recipe can also be used as a first course.

1 Crenshaw or honeydew melon
1 large cantaloupe
2 tbs. lime juice
2 tbs. honey
$\frac{1}{2}$ tsp. ground coriander
$\frac{1}{2}$ tsp. nutmeg
fresh mint sprigs, for garnish

Cut melons in half, remove seeds and scoop out round balls with a melon baller. In a small bowl, combine lime juice, honey, coriander and nutmeg. Pour dressing over melon balls, stirring to combine. Cover and refrigerate for 2 hours before serving.

ALMOND BISCOTTI

Biscotti are Italian cookies that are quite crisp and often dipped in coffee. Barley malt and concentrated fruit sweetener are natural sweet syrups that are used as substitutes for sugar because they take longer for the body to absorb. Find them in health food stores.

1/4 cup barley malt
1/2 cup concentrated. fruit sweetener
1/2 cup (1 stick) unsalted butter, melted
2 1/2 tbs. ground anise
1 tsp. almond extract

1 cup sliced almonds, toasted
3 large eggs
2 2/3 cups whole wheat pastry flour
1 1/2 tsp. baking powder

Spray a cookie sheet with nonstick cooking spray. In a large bowl, mix barley malt, fruit sweetener, butter, anise, almond extract and almonds together with a whisk. Beat in eggs. Then mix in flour and baking powder and blend thoroughly. Cover and refrigerate dough for 3 hours.

Heat oven to 350°. Shape dough into 3 flat loaves about 1 inch thick. Bake for 15 to 20 minutes. Remove loaves from oven and cut into 3/4-inch-thick diagonal slices. Lay slices cut sides up close together on cookie sheet. Return cookies to oven bake an additional 15 minutes. Cool cookies completely before storing in an airtight container.

LEMON POPPYSEED CAKE

Using natural fruit sweeteners and whole wheat pastry flour helps increase the absorption time, avoiding sugar spiking. Look for brown rice syrup and fruit sweetener in health food stores.

1/2 cup (1 stick) unsalted butter, softened
1/2 cup fruit sweetener
1/3 cup brown rice syrup
1/4 cup Splenda
3 eggs, separated
2 cup whole wheat pastry flour

1 1/4 tsp. baking soda
1 cup nonfat plain yogurt (or lemon yogurt)
2 tsp. pure lemon extract
1/2 cup poppyseeds
2 egg whites
1/4 tsp. cream of tartar

Heat oven to 350°. Grease and flour a 9-inch tube pan.

In a large bowl, using a mixer, cream butter, fruit sweetener, rice syrup and Splenda together until thoroughly mixed. Beat in egg yolks. Add flour and baking soda to creamed mixture alternately with yogurt. Mix in lemon extract and poppyseeds.

In a separate bowl, beat 5 egg whites with cream of tartar until whites are stiff but not dry. Fold 1/2 of the whites into the batter to lighten, then fold in the remaining whites. Pour batter into prepared pan and bake for 40 minutes or until golden. Cool completely before removing from pan.

PINEAPPLE MILLET PIE

Millet is a grain available at health food stores and stores carrying whole-grain products. Because millet is nearly 15% protein, is high in fiber and is alkaline-forming when digested, it is recommended for use in a low-carb diet even though its glycemic index is fairly high. This creamy pineapple pie may require a little more sweetener depending on your personal taste.

1½ cups plus 2 tbs. ground pecans, divided
2 tbs. melted butter
2 tbs. sugar or Splenda
1½ cups ricotta cheese
2 tbs. honey or Splenda
2 tbs. frozen pineapple-orange juice
    concentrate

1 can (8 oz.) crushed pineapple in juice,
    drained
¾ cup cooked millet
2 tsp. grated orange zest
1 tsp. vanilla extract
⅛ tsp. cinnamon

Heat oven to 350°. In a bowl, combine 1½ cups of the pecans with butter and sugar. Press this mixture onto the bottom and sides of a 9-inch pie pan, bake for 10 minutes. Set crust aside to cool. In a medium bowl, mix together ricotta, honey, juice concentrate, pineapple, millet, orange zest and vanilla with a spoon until smooth. Spoon this mixture into cooled piecrust. Mix cinnamon with the remaining 2 tbs. pecans and sprinkle on top. Refrigerate for 1 hour before serving.

GINGERSNAPS

The intense flavor of the ginger makes this cookie a candidate for low-sugar cooking. For a garnish, chop a little candied ginger into fine pieces and sprinkle on top before baking.

2 tbs. vegetable oil
3 tbs. molasses
1¾ cups barley flour or whole wheat pastry flour
½ tsp. baking soda
½ tsp. cinnamon
2 tsp. grated fresh ginger
⅓ cup apple juice concentrate

Heat oven to 350°. In a large bowl, combine oil and molasses. Stir in flour, baking soda, cinnamon, ginger and apple juice until well combined. Roll dough out ¼-inch thick and place on a greased cookie sheet. Bake for 8 to 10 minutes and remove from oven. Note: the cookie will harden when cool.

LEMON SOUFFLÉ

This delicious dessert would be great served with a little Lemon Sauce, *page 131.*

2 tbs. butter

2 tbs. flour

$\frac{1}{2}$ cup half-and-half

$\frac{1}{3}$ cup fresh lemon juice

$\frac{1}{3}$ cup sugar or Splenda

2 tbs. lemon zest

5 egg yolks

5 egg whites

$\frac{1}{8}$ tsp. cream of tartar

$\frac{1}{8}$ tsp. salt

Heat oven to 400°. Butter bottom and sides of a $1\frac{1}{2}$-quart soufflé dish and dust with sugar. Heat butter in a saucepan over medium heat, stir in flour and cook for 2 minutes. Remove from heat and stir in half-and-half. Return to heat and cook, stirring constantly, until mixture thickens. Remove pan from heat, beat in lemon juice, sugar, lemon zest and egg yolks. Set aside to cool. In a large bowl, using a mixer, beat egg whites until foamy. Add cream of tartar and salt and beat until stiff but not dry. Stir $\frac{1}{4}$ of the egg whites into milk mixture to lighten. Gently fold in remaining egg whites. Spoon batter into prepared soufflé dish and place in the middle of oven. Reduce heat to 375° and bake 35 minutes. Serve immediately.

PAVLOVA

Pavlova is a delicate meringue dessert named for a Russian ballerina. It is served with sweet-ened whipped cream and fresh slices of strawberry, raspberry, peach, or other fruit.

3 large egg whites
3 tbs. cold water
1/2 cup sugar
1/2 cup Splenda
1 tsp. white vinegar
1 tsp. pure vanilla extract
1 tbs. cornstarch
1 cup cream, whipped and sweetened, if desired
2 cups fresh sliced fruit

Heat oven to 300°. In a large bowl, using a mixer, beat egg whites until stiff, add water and beat for 1 minute. Add sugar, Splenda, vinegar, vanilla and cornstarch and beat for 10 minutes. Line a cookie sheet with parchment paper. Spread meringue mixture on parchment in a flat oval shape. Bake for 45 minutes. Cool the meringue to room temperature. Spread with whipped cream and top with fruit. Serve immediately.

MOCHA MOUSSE

This is a nice, light dessert which is low in sugar and high in protein. You may want to increase the cocoa powder or coffee granules to intensify the flavor.

1 cup ricotta cheese
$1/4$ cup plain yogurt
$1 1/2$ tbs. unsweetened cocoa powder
$1/4$ cup sugar
$1/4$ cup Splenda sugar
$1/2$ cup water
1 envelope unflavored gelatin

$1/2$–1 tsp. instant coffee granules
1 cup milk
1 tbs. coffee liqueur
$1/2$ tsp. pure vanilla or coffee extract
fresh mint sprigs, chocolate curls or chopped
toasted nuts, for garnish

In a food processor workbowl or blender container, combine ricotta cheese, yogurt and cocoa powder until smooth. In a saucepan, combine sugar, Splenda, water and gelatin. Set aside for 1 minute to soften gelatin. Cook over medium-low heat for 5 minutes. Stir in coffee granules and remove mixture from heat. Combine gelatin mixture with the ricotta mixture and refrigerate for 1 hour, stirring occasionally. With a mixer, beat chilled mousse to aerate, then spoon into dessert cups. Refrigerate 3 to 4 hours before serving. Decorate with garnish of choice.

PEACH AND BLUEBERRY COBBLER

Peach and blueberry flavors marry well. Fresh fruit is always preferred but frozen blueberries and unsweetened canned peaches can be substituted.

2 cups fresh blueberries
3 cups sliced peaches
1$\frac{1}{2}$ cups water
1$\frac{1}{4}$ cups packed brown sugar, divided
2 tbs. cornstarch
$\frac{1}{2}$ tsp. salt
1$\frac{1}{4}$ tsp. cinnamon, divided
$\frac{1}{2}$ tsp. nutmeg
1 pinch pepper
$\frac{1}{4}$ tsp. ground mace
$\frac{1}{2}$ cup whole wheat pastry flour
1 cup oats
$\frac{1}{4}$ cup ($\frac{1}{2}$ stick) butter
1 unbaked piecrust (9-inch)
sweetened whipped cream, for garnish

Heat oven to 350°. Place blueberries and peaches in a bowl. In a saucepan over high heat, bring water, 3/4 cup of the brown sugar, cornstarch, salt, 1 tsp. of the cinnamon, nutmeg and pepper to a boil, then reduce heat and simmer for 2 minutes. Pour over fruit and stir to combine. In a small bowl combine the remaining 1/2 cup brown sugar, remaining 1/4 tsp. cinnamon, mace, flour and oats. With a pastry cutter or 2 knives, cut in butter until mixture is crumbly. Pour fruit mixture in piecrust and sprinkle with oat mixture. Bake for 1 hour or until crumb topping is golden brown. Serve warm with whipped cream.

HAZELNUT CHERRY CLAFOUTI

Clafouti is similar to a large pancake baked with fruit inside. If fresh cherries are not available, canned cherries can be substituted.

½ cup chopped hazelnuts
1 tbs. flour
⅓ cup sugar or Splenda
2 eggs
3 egg yolks
⅔ cup heavy cream

1 pinch salt
1¼ cups pitted fresh cherries
1½ tbs. cherry liqueur
½ cup sliced toasted almonds
powdered sugar, for garnish
¾ cup heavy cream, whipped

Place hazelnuts and flour in a food processor workbowl or blender container and process until nuts are ground to a fine powder (do not overprocess). Transfer mixture to a bowl and, using a mixer, blend in sugar, eggs, egg yolks, cream and salt until well mixed. Cover and refrigerate overnight.

Heat oven to 350°. Butter a 9-inch pie pan. In a small bowl, mix cherries with liqueur. Pour ½ of the refrigerated batter into prepared pie pan, spread with cherry mixture and cover with remaining batter. Sprinkle with almonds and bake for 30 to 40 minutes or until golden brown. Sprinkle with powdered sugar and serve with whipped cream.

INDEX

Serve Creative, Easy, Nutritious Meals with nitty gritty® Cookbooks

100 Dynamite Desserts
The 9 x 13 Pan Cookbook
The Barbecue Cookbook
Beer and Good Food
Best Bagels are Made at Home
Best Pizza is Made at Home
Big Book of Bread Machine Recipes
Big Book of Kitchen Appliance Recipes
Big Book of Snacks & Appetizers
Blender Drinks
Bread Baking
Bread Machine Cookbook
Bread Machine Cookbook II
Bread Machine Cookbook III
Bread Machine Cookbook V
Bread Machine Cookbook VI
The Little Burger Bible
Cappuccino/Espresso
Casseroles
The Coffee and Tea Cookbook
Convection Oven Cookery
The Cook-Ahead Cookbook
Cooking for 1 or 2

Cooking in Clay
Cooking on the Indoor Grill
Cooking in Porcelain
Cooking with Chile Peppers
Cooking with Grains
Cooking with Your Kids
New Recipes for your Deep Fryer
The Dehydrator Cookbook
Edible Pockets for Every Meal
Entrees from Your Bread Machine
Extra-Special Crockery Pot Recipes
Fabulous Fiber Cookery
Fondue and Hot Dips
Fresh Vegetables
From Freezer, 'Fridge and Pantry
The Garlic Cookbook
Healthy Cooking on the Run
Healthy Snacks for Kids
From Your Ice Cream Maker
The Juicer Book
The Juicer Book II
Lowfat American Favorites
New International Fondue Cookbook

No Salt, No Sugar, No Fat
One-Dish Meals
The Pasta Machine Cookbook
Pinch of Time: Meals in Less than 30
    Minutes
Quick and Easy Low-Carb Recipes
Quick and Easy Pasta Recipes
Quick and Easy Soy and Tofu Recipes
Recipes for the Loaf Pan
Recipes for the Pressure Cooker
Rotisserie Oven Cooking
New Recipes for Your Sandwich Maker
The Sensational Skillet: Sautés and Stir-Fries
Slow Cooking in Crock-Pot,® Slow Cooker,
    Oven and Multi-Cooker
Simple Substitutions Cookbook
Soups and Stews
Tapas Fantasticas
The Toaster Oven Cookbook
Unbeatable Chicken Recipes
The Vegetarian Slow Cooker
New Waffles and Pizzelles
Wraps and Roll-Ups

For a free catalog, call: Bristol Publishing Enterprises.
(800) 346-4889
www.bristolpublishing.com